STORY SELLING

FOREWORD BY MARK VICTOR HANSEN

(CO-CREATOR OF CHICKEN SOUP FOR THE SOUL)

STORY SELLING

HOW TO PERSUADE PEOPLE TO THINK, FEEL, ACT, FOLLOW, BUY

DAN CLARK

HALL OF FAME SPEAKER
NEW YORK TIMES BEST SELLING AUTHOR
UNIVERSITY PROFESSOR

Story Selling
How To Persuade People To Think, Feel, Act, Follow, Buy

Copyright © 2022 Dan Clark.

ISBN: 979-8-88525-381-9

Table of Contents

Endorsement

By Zig Ziglar

"Let me introduce and endorse my friend, Dan Clark. I met him in 1982 and sponsored him into the National Speakers Association, where in 1987, he became the youngest ever to earn his CSP – Certified Speaking Professional designation in the history of the NSA. In the 25 years that I've known Dan, he has spoken an average of over 150 times a year to millions of people throughout the world. In recognition of his incredible reputation and success, Dan has been inducted into the Professional Speakers Hall of Fame.

"Dan is a marvelous human being, one who practices what he preaches, one who has his life in balance, one whose family is extraordinarily important to him, and one who is committed to bringing a message of hope and encouragement to any kind of audience he speaks to and/or for. Dan is one of the truly outstanding speakers in our world with a lot of good information that he delivers in an inspirational and humorous manner. He speaks and writes from his head and heart to your head and heart. Most importantly, he's a man of integrity. Every time I've shared the program with him, I realize it's more than cliché to say that what you see is what you get in Dan Clark. I encourage you to work with him. You'll be glad that you did."

—World Renown Motivational Teacher Zig Ziglar

Acknowledgments

Dedicated to my personal mentor, hero, and extraordinary mother Ruby Maughan Clark, who in 1975, introduced me to the transformational power of short stories. Because of her, I love to read, write, and speak, knowing I can change the world one story at a time!

To my dad, S. Wayne Clark, whom I love, admire and miss - who suggested that I should become the kind of speaker I enjoy listening to, which inspired me to become a storyteller.

To my professional mentor, hero, and friend Zig Ziglar – who sponsored me into the National Speakers Association and for over 25 years, personally coached me in the art and science of public speaking, story writing, and storytelling.

To the late great Og Mandino, from whom I took several writing classes, and to my special schoolteacher, Mrs. Smart, who saw something in me I did not see, and encouraged me to express myself through the power of the pen and the spoken word.

To Kelly (My Sweet KC Forever) for always being there for me through the 'thick of thin things,' believing in me when I didn't believe in myself!

To Danny and Natalie, Nikola and Ganes, McCall, Alexandrea, Sam and Liz, Debbie, and Paul and Kristi - who have created significant, entertaining, evocative, emotional experiences in my life that have molded me into the man I am, motivated to uncover the hidden messages and lessons found in everyday life, and sharing them in short stories, tall tales, message jokes, catchy anecdotes, emotional poems, hit song lyrics, and time-tested wisdom worth sharing with the world!

o smart, strong, talented, curious, creative, and extremely capable Aubree, Emma, Cora, Jack, and Luka – praying that they may continue to grow in knowledge, wisdom, understanding, and character-based confidence through the love of stories – especially those they read and hear from their 'Papa' who loves, respects and admires them more than words can express!

Foreword

By Mark Victor Hansen

Mastering the Fine Art of Storytelling - from the Master Storyteller!

Plato taught that whoever controls the narrative controls the future. Dan Clark is a rare, unique, and transformative storyteller and 'story seller' who proves Plato true! The best news for you is that the page-turning book you are about to read will not only edify you, but as you apply the principles, philosophies, and secrets that Dan shares, you will also become a great, wise, and insightful storyteller and 'story seller.'

Everyone has stories in them. Everyone loves to hear great stories. Few have ever listened to a master storyteller. Fewer have heard how to become an irresistible, compelling master at the creative and innovative art of storytelling.

Thanks to my great and inspiring friend, Dan Clark each of us can raise our ability to create and tell powerful, unforgettable stories. Dan is a consummate master, as such he makes the complex simple and can guide, lead, and advise you to master this most important of all money-making skills speaking, so sayeth the world's richest investor, Warren Buffett. Your life is about to become instantly more meaningful, significant, fulfilled, and 'full-thrilled' as you drink deeply of the wisdom, understanding, and insights of Dan Clark.

I have known and been a friend and colleague of Dan's for multiple decades. He is a master speaker, storyteller, writer, singer, leader, father, husband, and friend to all who hear and meet him. After I heard him at the National Speakers Association and heard him say that he spoke convincingly to teenagers - I immediately asked him to speak to my teenage daughter's school. He absolutely wowed the junior high kids and proceeded to wow the faculty and teachers at an in-service seminar and ended the day by giving all their parents hope and confidence that they were okay and their sons and daughters would grow up and do new wonders. It was exciting to hear Dan wax on poetically to thundering standing ovations at each of those three presentations - all done in one exhausting, non-stop day.

When Jack Canfield and I created the Chicken Soup for the Soul series, I loved Dan's great stories and appealed to him to write for us. He did. We happily published every story that he submitted. I have had the extraordinary pleasure of repeating many of his brilliant story contributions, whenever I speak - like *Puppy's For Sale.*

When my wife, Crystal and I discovered and decided that the difference between individuals having a little success and a vast amount of success was one thing only - the ability to ask effective and persuasive questions - we wrote *'ASK! The Bridge From Your Dreams to Your Destiny.'* The first person I called and asked for an interview about the art, science, and technology of *asking* was Dan Clark.

Without hesitation, he gave us a phenomenal story. I am thankful to say that every reader loves his story. The book keeps selling out everywhere and our publisher is elated that it keeps happening.

Some of the phenomenal benefits of storytelling and story-selling include:

- A way to help romance come alive whether you are single or married
- The opportunity to become universally loved, admired, and respected
- The possibility to fast-advance in your career with greater earning power
- The way to have more joy, happiness, fulfillment, bliss, and excitement in your life

You may ask yourself, why is my story important, meaningful, and worthy of sharing? If you are alive, God has a purpose and destiny for you. It emanates forth from your self-created story line. Solomon the richest man of all time, purportedly worth over four trillion dollars, answered wisely in *Psalm 72 that* your obligation is to be an *influencer of influencers*, with well-crafted, persuasively executed stories that sell.

My vision for you is that you read, dream about, and become a master storyteller and 'Story Seller.' As you do, attend one of Dan's seminars and be elevated to an even higher plateau of thinking, being, and becoming. I want to congratulate you in advance for embarking on this delightful, 'full-thrilling,' and grow-oriented journey.

Mark Victor Hansen
Co-creator of the *Chicken Soup for the Soul series*, *ASK* and *You Have A Book In You* - Author of 318 books, selling over 500,000,000 books worldwide!

Must Read Introduction

"Put it before them briefly so that they will read it, clearly so that they will understand it, forcibly so that they will appreciate it, picturesquely so that they will remember it, and, above all, accurately so that they may be wisely guided by its light." – *Joseph Pulitzer*

At the end of every day, every conversation, every personal and organizational branding strategy, every sales and marketing campaign, and every personal relationship boils down to a story!'

Whether your goal is to deliver the perfect wedding toast, wow clients at a business dinner, give a moving eulogy, ace a job interview, be a hit at parties, network at the highest levels, influence the affluent, change the world, or simply connect more deeply to those around you, stories are essential.

Apparently, you have decided to read this book because you agree and realize that being a great talker doesn't mean you're a great communicator. There's a difference between talking and teaching - between activity and accomplishment - between speaking at someone and to someone, versus *with* someone so they feel your words and internalize your message.

To achieve this deeper, most intimate level of communication requires that you master the art and science of storytelling. For this reason, I have compiled Twenty Chapters filled with the secrets to writing, editing, and telling congenial, gripping, engrossing, spellbinding, unforgettable stories - guaranteed to teach you how to:

- Persuade people to Think, Feel, Act, Follow, and Buy your beliefs, expectations, behavior, philosophies, products, and services

- Become a trusted advisor knowing no one wants to be sold but everybody will buy a compelling story
- Become more fascinating and inspirational to be around
- Perfect the fine art of persuasion and excellent communication
- Get paid to speak and publish your own book

By definition, 'Storytelling is the process of using fact and narrative to communicate something to your audience. Some stories are factual, and some are embellished or improvised to better explain the core message. Storytelling is an art form as old as time and has a place in every culture and society.'

Because everybody loves a good story, if you want to sell your product to customers, your vision to investors, or your ideas to the world, you've got to recognize the power and importance of great storytelling.

Grace Schulte wrote: "Storytelling is a timeless art – a way to share experiences, spark imagination, and connect with others on a deeper level. Whether you're telling a story to children before bed, sharing a memory with friends, or simply crafting a tale in your own mind, storytelling is usually a magical experience."

"Stories are a communal currency of humanity." – Tahir Shah

"The human species thinks in metaphors and learns through stories." – Mary Catherine Bateson

"Sometimes reality is too complex. Stories give it form and function." – Jean Luc Godard

"The stories we tell literally make the world. If you want to change the world, you need to change your story." – M. Margolis

"Stories transport people to another place." – J.K. Rowling

"Stories take the heart to places the mind can never go." – Dan Clark

Storytelling describes the social and cultural activity sometimes using improvisation, theatrics, or embellishment. Every culture has its own stories or narratives, which are shared as a means of entertainment, education, cultural preservation or instilling moral values. Historically, Storytelling, intertwined with the development of mythologies, predates writing. Some archaeologists believe that rock-art, cave-art, and petroglyphs may have served as religious rituals and a form of storytelling for many ancient cultures.

Storytelling has always been the best tool to communicate ideas, persuade others, and get what you want. The greatest speakers and teachers of all time have always been extraordinary storytellers. Stories are memorable. They are relatable. They are easier to recall and share with others. A great story stays with you because it brings to life the message through characters other than the storyteller. Especially when the storyteller doesn't 're-tell' the story – he/she 're-lives' it!

Starfish

A classic example is the familiar tale of the Starfish. A young girl was walking along a beach where thousands of starfish had been washed up during a terrible storm. When she came to each starfish, she would pick it up and throw it back into the ocean. People watched her with amusement.

She had been doing this for some time when a man approached her and said, "Little girl, why are you doing this? Look at this beach! You can't possibly save all these starfish. There are way too many for you to make a difference."

The girl seemed crushed for a moment. But suddenly, she smiled, bent down, picked up another starfish, and hurled it as far as she could into the sea. Looking the man square in the eyes, she quietly replied, "Made a difference for that one!"

When we hear this iconic story, it reminds us in an unforgettable way of the power we have over our perspective and ability to serve others if we so choose. Better still, when we tell this story it inspires others to join the little girl in throwing starfish back into the sea, until all of our family, friends, coworkers and teammates are saved.

Gandhi

When our message is to "seek counsel, not opinion,' the most effective way to communicate is to share a story:

A woman in India was upset that her son was eating too much sugar. No matter how much she chided him, he continued to satisfy his sweet tooth. Totally frustrated, she took her son to see his hero Mahatma Gandhi.

Mother reverently approached the great leader and respectfully explained, 'Sir, my son eats too much sugar. Would you please advise him to stop eating it?'

Gandhi thought, then told the mother and her son to come back in two weeks. Reluctantly she took the boy home.

Two weeks later she returned, son in hand. Gandhi motioned for them to come forward. He looked directly at the boy and said, 'Young man, you should stop eating sugar. It is not good for your health.'

The boy nodded and promised he would not continue this habit any longer. A bit irritated, the boy's mother asked Gandhi why he didn't tell him that two weeks ago?

Gandhi smiled, 'Mother, two weeks ago I was eating sugar.'

Can you see how in the context of a simple story, it is easy to illuminate the difference between one who gives you their opinion by telling you what to do, and one who counsels you by showing you what they are doing. Gandhi lived in such integrity that he would not allow himself to give advice unless he was living by it himself.

Power of Parables

Regardless of your religious tradition, we all can agree that Jesus was one of history's greatest teachers and used stories called 'parables,' to teach His messages. At the time it was a common form of teaching in Judaism.

In the case of Jesus' parables, many of his listeners were still contemplating their application well beyond their initial telling, often arriving at the meaning of the message on their own, as opposed to simply being told.

For Jesus, a parable was an earthly story with a heavenly meaning and a means of illustrating profound, divine truths. Stories such as these are easily remembered, the characters bold, and the symbolism rich in meaning. Jesus often employed many graphic analogies using common things that would be familiar to everyone (water, salt, bread, oil, sheep, light, pieces of silver) and their meaning was clear in the context of His teaching.

When it came time for Jesus to deepen His message and provide more explanation, He used parables because they contain great volumes of truth in very few words, are rich in imagery, are not easily forgotten, and are always relevant for every generation.

One of the most iconic examples is the 'Parable of the Ten Talents' regarding work, set in the context of investments. To paraphrase. A rich man traveling into a faraway country calls his own servants and delegates to them the management of his wealth, much as investors in today's markets do. He gives five talents (a large unit of money) to the first servant, two talents to the second, and one talent to the third 'to every man according to his several abilities.'

The servant with five talents 'traded with the same' and increased his talents to ten. The one with two increases his talents to four, but the third servant hides the money and earns nothing. When the rich man returns and asks for an accounting, the servant that had been given five reported a 100% return. Pleased, the rich man replies, 'Well done, thou good and faithful servant: thou hast been faithful over a few things, I will make thee ruler over many things: enter into the joy of thy lord.'

When the second servant reported his 100% return the rich man again replied, 'Well done, thou good and faithful servant… enter thou into the joy of thy lord.' Notice that although the sum totals were vastly different (ten and four), both servants received the exact same reward.

However, the rich man severely punishes the servant who did nothing, takes his one talent away, and gives it to the servant who had ten and 'cast the unprofitable servant into outer darkness.' Whoa!

Because of the way this centuries-old parable was crafted, it reminds us that storytelling reveals meaning without committing the error of defining it, showcasing five timeless entrepreneurial, business truths that are relevant today:

- Success is a product of our work.
- We are not all created equal and do not have the same talents as others – born with our 'several different abilities.'
- Competition against others can make us fearful and bitter. Competing against ourselves always makes us faithful and better.
- Those who are seeking significance serve others, not our own selfish purposes.
- We must take 100% responsibility for our results and will be held accountable.

For you and me in our time and place, the term 'storyteller' can refer to an oral and written description of an event, or movies, music, and dance, which bring understanding and meaning to human existence.

Storytelling was best described by Reynolds Price when he wrote:

'A need to tell and hear stories is essential to the species Homo sapiens – second in necessity apparently after nourishment and before love and shelter. Millions survive without love or home, almost none in silence; the opposite of silence leads quickly to narrative, and the sound of story is the dominant sound of our lives, from the small accounts of our day's events to the vast incommunicable constructs of psychopaths.'

For these reasons, I have written and compiled this book with one purpose in mind: to inspire you to believe and remember:

- Your life is not a life. It's a continuous collection of character-building experiences and individual stories, each one having a 'hello' and a 'goodbye' – one after the other in a sequential order that has made you the person you are today! Much like an American football game, which is a 60-minute contest, broken down into 60 to 70 individual plays, your life is the sum total of every 'one thing' (one play) you have thought and done, victories and defeats, successes and failures, sad, disappointing, discouraging, exhilarating, significant and fulfilling.

- The only way we can get better as the game goes on, and make the necessary adjustments to win the game, is to take the time to evaluate each 'play,' identify what we learned from it, and then implement the lessons to improve our performance before the game ends. These individual 'plays' are stories. Your life is a collection of thousands of stories. When you quantify them, you create a 'playbook' that you can refer to and share with others.

- Nothing in life happens 'to' you – it all happens 'for you' – to give you experience and mold and sculpt you into the complete person you were born to be. Everything happens for a reason. But it is your responsibility to determine what that reason is and evaluate the lesson learned so you can use it to change/heal/entertain and add value to our world!

- 'Your story is yours. But it's not yours to keep if it can help others get up and grow!' - Tony Rodrigues

Chapter One

Story Power

"The most powerful person in the room is the storyteller who sets the vision, values, and agenda of an entire generation that is to come."
– Steve Jobs

Beginning With the Message in Mind

I played American football for thirteen years when one day in a practice tackling drill I was injured, leaving me paralyzed for fourteen months. I went to sixteen doctors, fifteen of whom told me I would never get better. Now that I've recovered, I'm asked many questions, most of which I will answer when I share this complete 'Signature Story' later in the book.

For now, the key question I want to answer to get your juices flowing is: What took me so long to recover? Answer: I was asking the doctors how to get better - when I should have been asking myself why. Once we answer why, figuring out the how-to becomes clear and simple.

When we only focus on the What and How we only engage the head and brain. But when we add to that a passionate Why and a compelling Want, we connect the head with the heart, which makes our blood pump more rapidly, our brains fire and our muscles engage, which maximizes our performance!

In business, our 'why' is not to make a profit. That's a result. By 'why' I mean what's your cause? What's your purpose and belief? Why does your organization exist? Why do you get out of bed in the morning? And why should anyone care?

Sharing our 'why' changes us from a Transactional leader, manager, coach, parent, speaker/storyteller, communicating and connecting only in the 'head space' of information and logic, into a Transformational leader, manager, coach, parent, speaker/storyteller, communicating and connecting at both the head and heart level of relationships and emotion. Our 'why' is our story.

Simon Sinek teaches, "People don't buy what you do; they buy why you do it. What you do is simply proof of what you believe."

Bottom line. People are more motivated by a company's mission and vision than by the features and benefits of its products. For example, Apple is known for its mission to 'think differently' and challenge the status quo, rather than just selling computers. Airbnb's mission is to connect people so that they can feel like they belong anywhere, rather than just offering short-term rentals.

What we believe is our story!

eBay Selling Experiment

In 2009, a journalist by the name of Rob Walker, conducted a very famous experiment to find out if storytelling really is the most powerful tool in the persuasive process of sales. So, he went on his computer and purchased 200 cheap, frivolous objects from eBay. The average cost of the objects was about $.99 each.

Walker then sent a request to 200 authors for each of them to write a story about the individual object in the picture he sent. He affectionately called this experiment the 'Significant Objects Project.'

After all 200 authors had responded and sent him their stories, Rob went back on eBay and sold each of the 200 objects with the specific story attached in the description. His results were astounding!

A tiny figurine of a Horse's Head (shown below) was purchased on eBay for $1. When the story was added next to the photo it sold for $62. That is an increase in value of over 60%.

The Bunny Candle (shown below) was purchased for $3. When the story was added next to the photo it sold for $112.50 and will soon be on display in a prestigious Art Gallery in New York City!

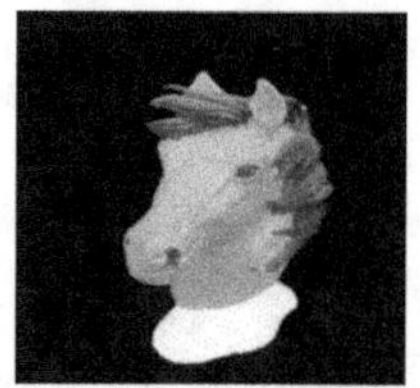 

Rob Walker bought the 200 objects on eBay for a total of $129. With the stories attached, he sold them on eBay for a total of $8,000! Welcome to the Art and Science of 'Story Selling!'

Psycho-Cybernetics

The first book I ever read on self-help, personal development, and the intriguing power of our minds is 'Psycho-Cybernetics' by Maxwell Maltz. Why? He related every example and researched data points through an illustrative story to make sure we readers understood what he was teaching. It was this book that made me realize the huge difference between talking and teaching - there is no communication in writing or speaking without total clarification and 100% understanding of the message being conveyed!

Stories are what make the truths and data points come alive! When we turn on the news, we don't remember the facts and figures – we remember the 'Interpretation' of the facts and figures. We want to know how the story relates to us and why we should act on its message.

What I figured out by reading 'in-between-the-lines' of Psycho Cybernetics is that knowledge is power, but it has no heart. We don't learn to know; we learn to do. All the information in the world is not going to make a person successful. It's like the guy who has three PhDs: one in philosophy, one in psychology, one in sociology – he doesn't have a job but at least he can explain why! Ha! Bottom line: Reason leads to conclusions, but it is emotion that leads to action. Emotion is created through storytelling!

Emotion does not exist in a vacuum by itself. It must be manufactured and triggered by ideas and beliefs. One of the best examples of this reality is an illustration from 'Psycho-Cybernetics':

Story: "Thoughts Are Things"

The human brain and nervous system are engineered to react automatically and appropriately to the problems and challenges in the environment. For example, a man does not need to stop and think that self-survival requires that he run if he meets a grizzly bear on a trail.

He does not need to decide to become afraid. The fear response is both automatic and appropriate. First, it makes him want to flee. The fear then triggers bodily mechanisms that 'soup' up his muscles so that he can run faster than he has ever run before. His heartbeat is quickened and adrenaline - a powerful muscle stimulant, is poured into the bloodstream. All bodily functions not necessary for running and escaping are shut down. The stomach stops working and all available blood is sent to the muscles. Breathing is much faster and the oxygen supply to the muscles is increased manyfold.

The challenge in this is that most believe this was an emotional response. No, it is not. The brain and nervous system that reacts automatically to the environment is the same brain and nervous system that tells us about the environment. The reactions of the man meeting the bear are commonly thought to be due to emotion rather than to ideas. It's an idea and flash of information received from the outside world and evaluated and interpreted by the mind that causes emotional reactions.

State of Mind

Our state of mind is made up of three parts: the brain, the mind, and ironically the body. Stubbing your toe causes you to feel pain. Your toe hitting the table leg is a physical event, and it causes your nerves to fire in a certain pattern, which sends a signal to your brain.

The question is: Are mental states identical to physical states? Is pain just the firing of those neurons in the brain? If so, your mind is nothing more than your brain. But if pain is something more than firing neurons, then there is room to conclude that your mind is something extra, something you have in addition to a body and a brain.

Bottom line. The body experiences the pain, the brain feels the pain, but it is the mind that interprets the pain and decides how it will affect you.

One of my favorite sayings is 'It's not what happens to you but what you do with what happens to you that makes or breaks you and defines who you are.' In this context, the body and the brain are what happens to you, and the mind is how you intentionally choose to either positively respond to what you value or negatively react to the emotional weather around you.

Because life is a story, our reality and ability to develop character, dream, set goals, pursue education, adapt to change, and be resilient, are all predicated on what stories we tell ourselves and others.

Story: "Why We Persevere"

Suppose you want to influence someone to buy a high-premium life insurance policy, and your presentation is a PowerPoint sales pitch on the features and benefits of the policy. In that case, you will seldom make a sale and remain an average Agent struggling to start and/or grow your business.

However, if you want to become a national sales champion you will become a master Story Seller!

My friend David Buchwald was an extremely successful financial advisor working out of New Jersey. Then, one day changed his reasons to persevere. On September 11, 2001, the World Trade Center Twin Towers in New York City were attacked. Nearly three thousand innocent lives were lost. Among the dead were fifty-one of David's clients whom he considered friends.

After the funerals, David delivered fifty-one multi-million-dollar death benefit checks to the heartbroken widows left behind.

I've shared the program with David, where he states how grateful he was that he refused to take 'no' for an answer! Thankful that he believed in his product and service so deeply that he relentlessly called back time and time again knowing the sale doesn't begin until the customer says 'no!'

Can you see how this story turns the heart and mind of a prospect into a buying client because they 'feel' the possible consequences of inaction and what a generous insurance policy would mean to a man's family if for some reason his life was taken early?

Story: "Spindletop"

While I was fighting back from a paralyzing football injury, I heard a recording by a motivational teacher by the name of Zig Ziglar. I only remember one story, but it was enough to change my life forever!

At the turn of the century, a farmer purchased a large farm in south Texas. Soon hard times hit, and he decided to sell some of his land to feed his family. The day his sign was posted a representative of an oil company came calling and explained that they believed there was oil on his property and if he would allow them to drill, they would pay him a royalty on every barrel they pumped out of the ground. He agreed.

The oil gushed from the ground with such force that it destroyed the wood derrick, introducing the world to 'Spindletop' – which became the most productive well in the history of the world! And… the man became an instant millionaire! Or did he?

Was he not a millionaire the day he purchased the land? The oil had always been there! He just didn't realize it! All he needed to do was drill deep enough to find the oil and get it out so he could use it!

In my confused and depressed condition, I was not emotionally able to absorb a medical or psychological solution. However, because Zig told a story that struck a chord with my predicament, his words inspired me to believe I had unrealized potential I could tap into! I metaphorically saw my body as the oil-rich land, my desire, discipline, and work ethic as my oil, and my mind and heart as the derrick to extract the oil that would fuel my recovery. The minute we get someone to believe the story we tell them; we can influence their thinking and behavior.

Story: "The Clark Credo"

I first experimented with the power of words when my mentor Zig Ziglar and I studied the lasting impact that 'affirmations' have on molding a person's attitude, beliefs, expectations, and behavior. When my wife was pregnant with our first child, Zig encouraged us to write a family creed to teach our new baby. When he was born, every night before I turned off the light, I would lean into his crib, and when I had eye contact, I repeated the following:

I'm smart, talented, and I never say never.
I'm wanted, important, lovable, capable and I can succeed.
I love music, I'm a great athlete and will get good grades in school.
The only person I need to be better than is the person I was yesterday.
So, I never say 'I can't' – I always say 'I can, I will.'
If I fall or get knocked down, I just get back up and go again.
If I spill or make a mistake, I learn why, say 'no big deal,'
and clean it up.

I love God and He loves me, so I treat others

> how they want to be treated –
> So, when we're apart, they always say:
> 'I like me best when I'm with you, I want to see you again!'

Every night I repeated this until Danny got old enough to start filling in a word here and there – until he could eventually repeat it word verbatim. Every night when I asked him, 'Who are you?' He would reply, 'I'm smart, talented, and I never say never. I'm wanted, important, ….."

We ended up having four children, and I repeated this nightly ritual, teaching the 'Credo' to each child. They are all adults now, and we are empty nesters filled with the joy and satisfaction that each of them turned out to be positive, kind, responsible, mentally strong, ethically straight, morally awake adults who are humble, grateful, and resilient.

Thankfully, none of them ever got into trouble; all were great athletes because they competed against what they were capable of, all got good grades in school, all learned from their mistakes, all are kind, and to this day, they always get back up when they fall, with a continual commitment to love God by keeping His Commandments.

Coincidence? No! Self is not discovered; self is created, and we proved it by actively participating in what went into our children's minds, hearts, and souls! As adults, all four children can still repeat the 'Credo' as it's been a continual source of strength when they need to do hard things - when they question if they are 'enough,' or when they simply need to feel a greater sense of belonging.

We now have five grandchildren, and I have taught each of them the 'Credo,' with the firm conviction that they, too, will become positive, kind, responsible, hardworking, resilient, God-loving teenagers and adults, who will eventually teach their children the 'Clark Credo.

Will you accept my challenge to write your own personal, family, and organizational 'Credos' to create stronger self-worth, kindness, mental toughness, and generational emotional prosperity?

Chapter Two

The Art of Storytelling

"In a world cluttered with lackluster messages, stories make us unforgettable! When we hear a story, our brainwaves synchronize with those of the storyteller, creating a deeper connection and validating why communication starts with 'getting on the same wavelength.'
– A. Rankin

I love a good story. The anticipation. The buildup of conflict. The climax and the payoff. As you experience the journey through the hero's eyes, you might be left laughing, crying, or nodding your head in agreement.

Creator of TED Talks, Chris Anderson, writes: 'As a leader or as an advocate – public speaking and storytelling is the key to unlocking empathy, stirring excitement, sharing knowledge and insights, and promoting a shared dream. It's the ability to captivate an audience with *presentation literacy* - the superpower to pitch your ideas and sell products.

The New Leadership Role

People are 22 times more likely to internalize a story than to remember bullet points of facts or figures. Why? A well-crafted and engaging story defines your brand's purpose and reinforces your value proposition, driving internal and external transformational outcomes.

In Jacob Morgan's incredible book, The Future of Work, he asks if in 2022 and beyond, will companies be about AI (Artificial Intelligence) and automation, or about the creation of more socially responsible 'human' organizations.

Surely, we cannot allow technology to take over every phase of our lives to where we go to a doctor's office and there is no human being. Where all we get is a recording that says, "If your pain is below the waist press 3." Surely the Catholic Church is not going to automate confessions and make us dial in at "1-800 Fess Up" - with a recording that says, "If you are into bigamy press 2. If you're worshipping the devil press 666." Ha!

The companies and organizations that will thrive and dominate their industries now and, in the future, are those who overcompensate high tech with high touch, exemplifying to their employees and customers that technology is simply a tool and why and how we use it is a choice.

It's been proven that Artificial Intelligence can do a better job at analytics, strategy, and decision-making than a human can. But 'AI' cannot motivate or engage people. Only inspiring people can inspire people to motivate themselves! This means the only role left for a leader is to focus most of our time on igniting in others the mindset, heart-set, and skill sets that only human beings possess: purpose-driven passion, empathy, and respect. The most valuable intelligence is Not Artificial!

Transference of Trust

The definition of leadership, management, team building, coaching, educating, parenting, and civil service is the 'transference of trust.' We transfer trust by sharing our stories. Especially in the world of sales — which everybody in the world is engaged in!

Before we can ever get anyone to trust us enough to date, love, marry, or purchase a product or service, we first need to showcase our character and values in the form of our experiences and stories.

When we get to know one another's stories, we find common ground and shared beliefs where we connect and exchange the deepest level of trust that bridges the gap from stranger to friend. Professionally, we transform our value proposition from a 'sales pitch' to a 'Serve Pitch,' from trying to sell something to being a trusted advisor on what is best for them to buy!

Because sales is about the 'transference of trust, it is critical to embrace the research of the National Sales Survey Analytics Report:

- 44% of sales professionals quit after the first sales call.
- 24% quit after the second call.
- 14% quit after the third call.
- 12% quit after the fourth sales call.

94% of sales professionals quit by the 4th sales call. Yet the survey shows 85% of our sales are closed between the 5th and the 12th sales call!

This means that we need to make ourselves more compelling to talk to, more fascinating to be around, and more qualified to learn from, so our prospects and potential customers trust us enough to invite us into their inner circle five to twelve times until it's time to close the deal!

When we only live an ordinary life we can only tell ordinary stories! We stand out in our profession and in every situation when we don't just teach what we know. We teach who we are, how we live, and what we've done, keeping us fresh, relevant, and significant to hang out with!

When it comes to presentations, most sales presentations try to cram graphs and overwhelming details into a PowerPoint slide deck to convince the prospect with information. But in Story Selling you never 'sell past the close!' You share the info and tell the story until they 'feel' they should close themselves on the deal!

Story: "Who Are You - Really?"

One day I was walking in the mall with a friend when someone bumped into him, spilling his cup of coffee on the floor. I asked him what happened, and he said, 'I spilled my cup of coffee.' I countered, 'No, you spilled what was in your cup. Had you had juice in your cup, you would have spilled juice. We can only spill what's inside our cup.'

When life bumps into us, if we are negative - what spills out is anger, blaming, and complaining. If we are positive – what spills out is forgiveness, empathy, and love. You can surgically remove the stripes from a tiger and it's still a tiger. You can move to a different city, but no matter where you go, there you are. Relocating doesn't change much.

If you and I were roommates in college and we decided to wake up every morning at 6 am and go to the gym to work out for an hour and then study for an hour before our day got underway, we would be merely changing our behavior to push each other. But if You wake up every morning at 6 am, work out hard in the gym, and study for an hour regardless of whether I do or not, that is your true 'nature' – that is who you really are! You are pushing yourself - not because it is expected by others, but because it is demanded of yourself!

Story: "Are You All In?"

When you're asked to teach the difference between sympathy (feeling for someone) and empathy (feeling with someone) share a story:

For a month, a local businessman came to the Marriott Hotel lobby restaurant every Wednesday to hold a business meeting with a customer. One day, he showed up with his 10-year-old son. The restaurant Manager asked him, what was the special occasion?

The boy excused himself to use the lobby washroom. Dad explained that it was not a special occasion, but that his son had just been diagnosed with stage four cancer and was in for the battle of his life. So, they checked into the hotel, went shopping, and returned to take a dip in the pool, order room service, and watch a movie.

Dad explained that his son knew the medicine was going to make his hair fall out and wanted to shave his head that night to remind him that he was in control of the cancer, refusing to let the cancer control him. If you were his dad, what would you have done?

Obviously, Dad shaved his head too! Dad then asked the Manager if he would please let his restaurant staff know what was going on so that when he and his son showed up for breakfast with bald heads, no one would gawk or ask what happened to their hair. The Manager promised he would. In the morning when dad and his son showed up for breakfast, the two 17-year-old young men who came to take their orders had shaved their heads that night too!

Story: "No Child Dies Alone"

If you are the CEO of a Healthcare System and want to inspire people to come to your hospital for their medical needs, you share extraordinary patient experiences so they believe it could also happen to them!

For three years my wife and I volunteered at the Primary Children's Hospital. On Sunday mornings we visited patient rooms to invite the families to join us for a 30-minute non-denominational fellowship service to give and receive strengthening support. On our first day, we met a boy battling Cystic Fibrosis and invited his mom and grandparents to the devotional. After the meeting, Grandpa told us this story:

Last week his daughter (the mom of his grandson) left the hospital room to go to the pharmacy. Soon she passed by a young girl. Realizing the hospital had a 'buddy system' where no child was to be alone, the mom confronted the girl asking where her 'buddy' was.

The girl pointed down the hall and said, "I'm going to get him now!'

Mom took five more steps but immediately turned to check on her again. The girl was gone! She had disappeared, vanished, with no doors in the hallway. Baffled, Mom hurried to the pharmacy and quickly returned to her son's room. Sadly, the parents of the boy in the room next to her were in the hall sobbing and explained that their son had just passed away right after she left. Mom calculated that it was the exact time she had passed the girl in the hall, 'going to pick up her buddy.'

With tears in his eyes, Grandpa then stated, 'Angels walk these halls. No child dies alone in this sacred Children's Hospital!'

4 Truths – 3 Power Phrases – 2 Questions

We 'prime' a pump before we can draw water from a well. To create maximum impact as storytellers, we must also 'prime' ourselves to deliver the story at the same level of excellence that created it.

We do this by embracing four truths:

Four Truths

People buy with emotion and then justify with logic.

Sell the transformation, not the product.

It's easier to sell an offer that solves a pain than one fulfilling a desire.

Stories provide 'Social Proof' of Credibility, Possibility and Usability.

Once the storyteller is in this mindset, we can transfer it to the reader or listener by prefacing our story with one of three power phrases or by asking one of two questions.

Three Power Phrases

"I Need Your Help With Something." (making people want to immediately assist you.

"Just Imagine If…" (activating the brain's Visualization Center, bypassing logical resistance, and making your suggestions feel like they are their own ideas).

"You Are Probably Wondering Why…" (creating an open loop they need to close, forcing them to pay attention to what you say next).

Two Questions that Seek a 'No'

Instead of asking, "Do you mind if I propose an idea?" Ask, "Are you against me sharing an idea?"

As a speaker (with tongue in cheek), instead of saying, "Do you have a few minutes to talk?" Ask, "Is now a bad time to talk?" Ha!

In this way, the 'Do you Agree' becomes 'Do you disagree?' 'Is this a good idea?' becomes 'Is this a bad idea?'

By seeking a 'no,' you address objections that create clarity, build trust, and open conversations that show you understand, converting you from a salesperson into a 'Sales Assistant' and Influential Leader.

Authentic Communication

Once we know who we are, research shows that we connect and convert others to our way of thinking when we use Three Key Elements:

- Authority: your experience makes people do what you say (Tony Robbins, David Goggins, Gary V, Ben Shapiro).
- Compassion: makes people trust you, confide in you, and ask for advice (Jordan Peterson, Ed Mylett, Jay Shetty, Brene Brown).
- Entertainment: makes people pay attention to you (Russell Brunson, Brendon Burchard, Mel Robbins, Lewis Howes).

There is no good or bad communication style – just right or wrong based on your personality and which of the three elements is natural for you. If you try to speak from a place of Authority (command and control) and it's not really you, no matter how Compassionate or Entertaining you are, people will never buy from you. If you try to show Compassion (example and collaboration) and it's not really you, it doesn't matter how much Authority you project, or how Entertaining you are, people will not trust you because they sense something is 'off.' If you try to be Entertaining (popular and relational) and that's not really you, it doesn't matter how much Authority or Compassion you convey, people will not pay attention to you.

The most effective influencers initially connect as their 'true nature' selves in their primary communication style. However, when they are authentically Authoritative, they can't help but also manifest Compassion and be Entertaining. If they are authentically Compassionate or Entertaining, they can't help but manifest Authority.

The most successful, significant, respected, and admired people in the world use all three elements and communication styles to accelerate the 'transfer of trust,' turning leadership into influence and connection into conversion.

Chapter Three

The Essence of Storytelling

"Upon the fields of friendly strife are sown the seeds that upon other fields, on other days, will bear the fruits of victory – learning that the three hallowed words Duty, Honor, Country reverently dictate what you ought to be, what you can be, what you will be, sustained by the experiences you've lived and the conviction of your soul."
- General Douglas MacArthur

You Are the Message

When we meet someone for the first time, and flippantly ask them to tell us about themselves, most of the time they report: 'I'm a soldier, an entrepreneur, corporate exec, wife, mother, husband, father, financial advisor, realtor, speaker, author, coach, etc.' However, this is just 'what' they do, not 'who' they are! Who they *really are* is courageous, trustworthy, loyal, helpful, friendly, courteous, kind, caring, obedient, cheerful, brave, clean, reverent, positive, productive, passionate, creative, ambitious, resilient, respectful, empathetic, forgiving, unconditionally loving, non-judgmental, inclusive, grateful, and humble.

Before we can write a compelling inspirational story or powerful, unforgettable speech, we must first live a compelling, inspiring life! Before we can be extraordinary communicators and admired influencers, we must spend more time preparing ourselves to speak than we do preparing a presentation or keynote speech! This is the only way we can get people to choose us instead of just somebody who does what we do!

In our personal and professional lives, and especially on the stage as a speaker, we don't attract who we want to like us and embrace us. We attract who we are and connect only with those who trust us based not on what we know, but on how we live and why we do what we do. Our professional message can't be about a formula or strategy until it's about our integrity and why we believe what we believe based on our eyewitness experience.

For this reason, whenever someone asks me how they can become a professional motivational speaker, I always ask them what their compelling, life-changing message is. If they struggle to answer, I help them by asking four deeply introspective questions:

- What would you drive five hours to teach somebody for free?
If they say they wouldn't, they could never be a professional speaker because it's not a job, it's a 'calling' to embrace the 'Privilege of the Platform.'

- If you had one hour to live - what is the single, most significant, bottom-line message you feel compelled to share with the world as your 'Last Lecture?'

- Do you realize that people don't relate to your perfections; they relate to your imperfections? So, how vulnerable are you willing to be? **Remember, to love who you are, you cannot hate the experiences that shaped you!**

- What is the single most significant experience you have had that powerfully illustrates your transformational message and earns you the right to teach it?

"Signature Story"

In the world of public speaking, we refer to this as a 'Signature Story,' which you need to include in every speech because it reveals this 'Last Lecture' message that illuminates who you are and what you believe.

Your ability to make a maximum impact with every listener: 1 on 1, 1 on 10 in a board room, or 1 on 10,000 in an arena, drastically increases when you can sift through the many experiences in your life and uncover your 'Signature Story' – that one personal, intimate experience that stands out above the rest that contains your life-changing solutions so everybody leaves you saying, 'I like me best when I'm with you, I want to see you again?'

We can teach, counsel, and inspire others with our experiences, but we can never coach or mentor them in the steps of resiliency unless we have actually done it! No one will listen to our counsel if we have not personally experienced the physical pain, emotional devastation, spiritual questioning, and mental toughness that taught us the steps required to recover.

To illustrate, let me share one of my favorite stories that illustrates the power of self-belief and preparation. In the Old Testament Book of Judges Chapter Seven, we learn how Gideon defeated the Midianites.

"Early in the morning Gideon and all his 32,000 men camped at the waters of Herod preparing to go into battle. God told Gideon, 'You have too many men. I cannot deliver Midian into their hands, or Israel would boast against me: 'My own strength has saved me.' Now announce to the army that anyone who trembles with fear may turn back and leave Mount Gilead. So, 22,000 men left, while 10,000 remained.

But God told Gideon, 'There are still too many men. Take them down to the water and I will thin them out for you there. Separate those who lap the water from their cupped hands from those who kneel to drink like a dog.' Surprisingly, only 300 of them appropriately drank from cupped hands.

Then God told Gideon, 'With the 300 men that lapped from their hands I will save you and give the Midianites into your hands. So, Gideon sent the rest of the Israelites home but kept the 300 who valiantly fought to win the battle.

To be a passionate, credible storyteller and transformational speaker, not only do you need to believe that Gideon would have chosen you as one of the special, unique, and extraordinary 300, but you must live in a way that others will choose to trust your experience, believe in themselves, and follow your 'battle strategy' for the same reasons.

Speaker Triangle

In my comprehensive textbook on Speaking titled: Speak Like A Pro - The Art and Science of Significant Public Speaking – I share my 'Speaker Triangle' that illuminates the three questions everybody craves the answers to:

- Why Should I Listen To You?
- Can I Do It Too?
- How Do I Do It?

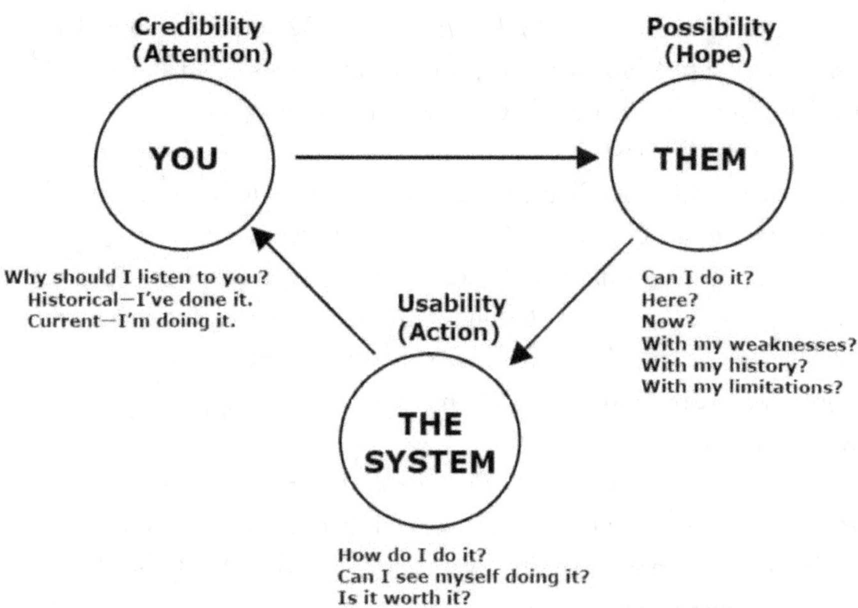

Although I mentioned the following story in Chapter Two, let me fill in some intimate details so you can analyze if the structure and presentation of the story answer these three questions.

Why Should I Listen to You?

One day during my American football practice, the coach whistled "go," and another player and I ran full speed into each other in a violent head-on collision, and we slammed to the ground. I lay there in shock, with a sharp, piercing burning pain shooting through my body. My eye drooped and my speech slurred (which momentarily returned). I had compressed my neck, suffered a grade-two concussion, severed the axillary nerve in my right deltoid, my right side was numb, and my arm dangled helplessly at my side. That night I perspired, threw up, and cried myself to sleep.

For the next fourteen months, I was paralyzed - both physically and emotionally. My heart was broken, my dreams were shattered, and my successful and promising career came crashing down. I went to sixteen doctors, fifteen of whom told me I would not get better, and I spiraled downward until I thought I hit rock bottom.

Now that I've recovered, I'm frequently asked Four Questions:

1. What do you mean you 'thought' you hit rock bottom? Answer: No matter how bad or tough it gets, nobody ever hits rock bottom. We

hit rock foundation - we hit rock belief – we hit the baseline core values and governing principles on which we were raised.

2. Why did I go to so many doctors? Answer: I kept going from doctor to doctor until I found one who *believed* I would get better – who turned probability into possibility thinking, explaining, 'Knowledge is power, but it has no heart. We don't learn to know, we learn to do. All the information in the world is not going to make a person successful. It's like the guy who has three PhD's: one in philosophy, one in. psychology, one in sociology – he doesn't have a job but at least he can explain why! Ha! Bottom line. Reason leads to conclusions, but it is emotion that leads to action!

3. What took me so long to recover? Answer: I stayed physically paralyzed for fourteen months because I was asking the wrong questions. I was asking the doctors how to get better when I should have been asking myself, 'Why?' Once we answer 'why,' figuring out the 'how' becomes clear and simple. Once I stopped focusing on having fame and chasing fortune and started focusing on my real purpose and becoming whole, I was able to persevere and do the hard things required to let go of my past and recreate my identity.

I stayed emotionally paralyzed until I realized there is a giant difference between being depressed and being disappointed and discouraged; learning that most people who claim they are depressed are actually experiencing 'H.A.L.T.S. – Hungry, Angry, Lonely, Tired or Sad.

When we are experiencing any one of these emotionally debilitating conditions, we can't feel, listen, focus, love, or forgive. I realized that to climb out of the darkness and once again embrace the light, I needed to embrace the fact that exhaustion is acceptable; falling is acceptable; puking is acceptable; crawling is acceptable; blood, sweat, and tears are acceptable; heartache and discouragement are acceptable; but whining, complaining, blaming, and quitting are not!

When I finally got tired of tolerating less than I deserved, I locked myself in my room until I had raised my right hand above my head. It took me seven hours! The next day it only took me five hours, so I was making daily, incremental, consistent progress! When I could finally lift my arm ten times, I took my rehab to the gym. Twenty months after my accident, I had fought my way back to a 95% recovery!

4. What are the lessons I learned that apply to Business Growth and Building a Winning Team? Answer: The secret to growth and achieving greatness is taking small steps. It's a commitment to 1% daily improvement, which, over time, creates a separation between you and your competitors in personal value and creating a customer experience.

Confidence comes through Preparation. So, when the game is on the line, I'm not asking myself to do something that I have not done hundreds of times before! When I prepare, I know what I'm capable of doing, because I've put in the work to improve myself 1% every day!

Most importantly, I learned and now teach the significance of Self-discipline, which makes us relentless, fierce Competitors.

Discipline is doing the right thing, the right way, at the right time – because it's expected by a leader or coach. However, Self-discipline is manifested in two ways: You have something you're supposed to do, you don't want to do it, but you get yourself to do it anyway. And, you have something you are not supposed to do, you want to do it, but you refuse to do it – because it's demanded of yourself!

Bottom line. Self-discipline simplifies life into two decisions: Feelings and Choices. Will you just do what you 'Feel' like doing? Or, will you 'Choose' to do what you need to do, because you need to do it?

Which makes you a relentless 'Competitor.' You see, there is a huge difference between an athlete who plays hard and one who is a competitor. If you play hard in basketball, you dive for a loose ball. If you are a competitor, you dive for the loose ball and make sure you get it! If you play hard, you box out your man. If you are a competitor, you box him out the entire game and don't let him get a single rebound!

Every company and team has employees and players who are disciplined and work and play hard! The championship organizations that consistently win have the most Self-disciplined, fierce competitors!

Story: "U2 Eternity"

When I am asked to speak on vision, perspective, and redefining what's possible, I share the following insane adventure to build my credibility:

A few years ago, on October 22 and 23, I had the rare opportunity to soar to the edge of space in a U2 reconnaissance aircraft. I trained for two months to lose 29 pounds, arrived on the base for a flight physical and day of orientation, was fitted into my 130-pound space suit, introduced to my Commander, and boarded the aircraft to rapidly climb to 17 miles (27 kilometers) above the earth.

For 5 hours, I sat in the sounds of silence, looking at the breathtaking curvature of the earth, gazing into the endless blackness of the universe, pondering eternity and my place in it, with a sudden comprehension of Ralph Waldo Emmerson's words: "The mind once stretched can never return to its original dimensions."

Overcome with emotion I teared up as an eyewitness to the words of Einstein, "Although the concept of a Master Organizer is complex, we must embrace the mindset of a child who walks into a library and says surely someone must have written all these books." Suddenly, it was obvious that we are more than mere mortal beings living on a small planet for a short season, 'called' to do something significant!

When we landed, I clamored to read the writings of world-renowned scientist Werner von Braun, the father of NASA, who was a devout believer in God and gave a science-based, theologically sound explanation of the order in the universe and how obeying its 'operational equation' will minimize mistakes and simplify our journey in mortality.

Creation/Organization of the Universe

The universe was organized and is governed by a set of irrevocable laws. Universal Laws include gravity, mathematics, physics, thermodynamics, aerodynamics, harvest, resonant attraction, and relativity.

When we obey a specific law, we reap a specific reward. When we disobey a specific law, we suffer a specific consequence. This makes Obedience the highest law of the universe. All other laws are governed by it.

To test our Obedience, the Master Organizer God gave us at least two or more choices in every aspect of our existence with the gift of Free Agency so we can always choose to obey of our own volition. This means obedience is what protects our Agency. If you disagree, visit a prison full of inmates who made bad choices and misused their Agency.

To guarantee our Agency, God allowed an Opposition in All Things: We have darkness to appreciate the light. Sickness to appreciate health. Justice to appreciate mercy. Captivity to appreciate freedom. Mistakes to appreciate forgiveness. Fear to appreciate faith. Corruption to appreciate in corruption. Death to appreciate the sanctity of life.

Because we are human, and God knew that with an Opposition in all things we would be tempted to disobey and misuse our Agency, He instilled in each of us an inherent ability to discern right from wrong, good from evil. We commonly call this ability our 'Conscience.'

Which means our Conscience will never fail us. Only our desire to follow it decreases as we continue to disobey universal law and do the wrong thing.

Can I Do It Too?
Story: "Parable of the Kite"

One day a father and his young son were in a park flying a kite. Dad asks him what holds the kite up in the sky. The boy answers, "The wind." Dad explains, "No, the string holds the kite up in the sky." His son counters, "No, the string holds the kite down." Dad smiles, "If you think so, let go of the string."

When the boy let go of the string, the kite fluttered from the sky. As the wind blew the kite wherever it decided to, the boy chased the string until he caught it. When he grabbed hold of the string, the kite again climbed skyward to be everything it was made to be.

In this parable, the *Kite* represents his (your) dream, desired result.

The *Wind* represents opposition—the economy, interest rates, competition, lack of capital investment, negative co-workers, and debt.

The *String* represents the rules, principles, and universal laws that must be obeyed to control the Kite dream against the opposition.

The boy *Holding Tightly to the String* represents him obeying his dad (boss, coach, or person in authority.

The boy *Letting Go of the String* represents him succumbing to the enticements of others and experiencing the consequence of disobedience as he watches the kite blow away.

The boy *Chasing the String* represents him listening to his conscience, realizing he should not have obeyed a person because they will eventually let us down. He should only obey the law and those who do!

The boy *Once Again Holding Tightly to the String* represents that he no longer needs supervision to fly his kite because he is disciplined to obey!

Most significantly, he has now experienced the blessing of 'forgiveness,' realizing that no matter how many times we let go of the string, we can always catch it again, and through self-motivation fueled by self-discipline, we can restore trust in ourselves and regain the trust and confidence from others that immediately put our life back on track!

How Do I Do It?

This 'Usability' How-To System helps us all pinpoint which part of the Parable is causing our pain: Is our dream 'Kite' not clearly defined? Is it the Opposition 'Wind' that's holding us back? What specific fear/obstacle/challenge do we need to face and overcome: bad attitude, lack of confidence, emotional support, financial assistance? Which specific universal law 'String' have we let go of and are currently disobeying? Who and what negative influences should we avoid?

Chapter Four
The Science of Storytelling

"Investing in public speaking and storytelling skills can increase a person's value by 50%." – Warren Buffet

As I studied Leo Widrich's research, it became clear that a good story can make or break a presentation, article, or conversation. But why is that?

We all enjoy a good story, whether it's a novel, a movie, or simply something one of our friends is explaining to us. But why do we feel so much more engaged when we hear a narrative about events?

It's quite simple. If we listen to a PowerPoint presentation with boring bullets and graphs, a certain part of the brain gets activated. Scientists call this Broca's area and Wernicke's area. Overall, it hits our language processing parts in the brain, where we decode words into meaning. And that's it. Nothing else happens.

When we are being told a story, things change dramatically. Not only are the language processing parts in our brain activated, but any other area in our brain that we would use when experiencing the story's events are too.

If someone tells us about how delicious certain foods are, our sensory cortex lights up. If it's about motion, our motor cortex gets active: Metaphors like 'The singer had a velvet voice' and 'He had leathery hands' roused the sensory cortex. Then, the brains of participants were scanned as they read sentences like 'John grasped the object' and 'Pablo kicked the ball.' The scans revealed activity in the motor cortex, which coordinates the body's movements.

A story can put your whole brain to work. Yet it gets better: When we share our stories that have shaped our thinking and way of life with others, we can also have the same effect on them. The brains of the person telling a story and listening to it can synchronize.

Evolution has wired our brains for storytelling – how to make use of it. Now all this is interesting. We know that we can activate our brains better if we listen to stories. The still unanswered question is: Why is that? Why does the format of a story, where events unfold one after the other, have such a profound impact on our learning?

The simple answer is this: We are wired that way. A story, if broken down into the simplest form, is a connection of cause and effect. And that is exactly how we think. We think in narratives all day long, regardless of whether it's about buying groceries, being more efficient at work, or explaining why we are late to our spouse. We make up short stories in our heads for every action and conversation. Research shows personal stories and gossip make up 65% of our conversations.

Whenever we hear a story, we want to relate it to one of our existing experiences. That's why metaphors work so well with us. While we are busy searching for a similar experience in our brains, we activate a part called 'insula,' which helps us relate to that same experience of pain, joy, or disgust.

Everything in our brain is looking for the *cause-and-effect* relationship of something we've previously experienced. The next time you struggle with getting people on board with your projects and ideas, simply tell them a story, where the outcome is that doing what you had in mind is the best thing to do.

A big idea alone will not fuel innovation. Marketing alone will not generate customers. Vision and products need stories that take people on a journey that changes how they think, feel, and act. When we tell stories that have shaped our thinking and way of life, the brains of those listening to us synchronize with our brains at a deeper level of connected understanding.

In an environment where highly connected customers communicate their 'likes' and dislikes at the push of a button, organizations are challenged to distinguish your value proposition as fresh, relevant and your brand clearly differentiated.

When you know how the 'narrative' affects brain chemicals that shape how you react or respond in every situation, how others view who you are, what you do, and why they should follow your lead, trust you as a partner, or buy your products and services, you can create the competitive advantage in the marketplace, maximize your influence in every presentation and accelerate their decision making.

The Biology of Motivation and Resilience

In Chapters One and Three, I shared my 'Signature Story' and purposefully left out the brain-science part to describe it here. As you recall, I stayed paralyzed for fourteen months because I was asking the doctors how to get better. When I finally asked myself 'why,' my rehabilitation process accelerated. How?

My recovery was not a 'raw-raw' motivational 'you can if you think you can,' mind over matter process. It was based on science and the physiologically proven fact that the 'why I do what I do' and 'my wanting to do it' exist in the limbic part of the brain that controls my feelings and decision-making. The 'what to do' and 'how to do it' exist in the neocortex part of the brain that controls my rational thought and my language.

Notice that how we feel and how we describe it reside in two different parts of the brain, which is why it's difficult to fully express everything we really want to say about gratitude, service, and love. As I mentioned in the beginning of the book, when we only identify a *what* and a *how*, we only engage the brain. However, a clearly defined *why* coupled with a compelling *want* (goal) has a huge impact on behavior because they engage both the head and the heart.

Yes, the brain is powerful. Napoleon Hill teaches in Think and Grow Rich: 'Thoughts are Things! We can literally change the way someone behaves by simply triggering the right brain chemical at the right time for the right reason to subconsciously influence them to embrace what we are saying/selling. All we must do is master our knowledge of the six major brain chemicals.

Six Brain Chemicals Change Our Behavior

Adrenaline

Is the *"Accelerator Drug."* When you need your people to Fire up, Rise to the Occasion, Hustle, and Access a 'second wind/extra effort' - you tell a story that releases Adrenaline, triggered by sudden changes, startling beliefs, and situations with a message to fight or flee.

Adrenaline is the *"Urgent Response / Muscle Stimulator,"* triggered for only 30 to 120 minutes through fear or sudden clarity of purpose.

Endorphin

Is the *"Motivational Drug."* When you need your people to be resilient and persevere - you tell a story that releases Endorphin – that is triggered with humor, and a message of pushing beyond physical limits, so they believe they can do it too.

Endorphin is the *"Pain Killer"* triggered through Laughter and Exercise.

Dopamine

Is the *"Performance Drug."* When you need your people to improve performance and accomplish a huge goal - you tell a story that releases

Dopamine – that is triggered by self-interest, which allows them to "check a box" that they can/should do it too.

Dopamine is the *"Reward Chemical"* triggered through Completing a task, Doing Self-Care Activities, Eating Food, and Celebrating Little Wins.

Serotonin

Is the *"Recognition Drug."* When you need to strengthen the bond, attachment, and loyalty required to retain your best people - you tell a story that releases Serotonin, triggered when you make them swell with pride, and feel valuable and needed.

Serotonin is the *"Mood Stabilizer"* triggered by: Meditation, Running, Sun Exposure, Walking in Nature, Swimming, and Cycling.

Oxytocin

Is the *"Love Drug."* When you need to strengthen trust and connect with internal and external customers - *you* tell a story about service before self that releases Oxytocin, triggered through smiling, eye contact, shaking hands, and understanding.

Oxytocin is the *"Relationship Hormone"* triggered by: Giving a Compliment, Shaking or Holding Hands, Hugging, Holding a Baby, and Playing with a Pet.

Cortisol

Is the negative, toxic *"Stress Drug"* – released when you tell a story that makes someone feel guilty, bad, and unworthy. Cortisol is the *"Energy-Sucking Hormone"* that stays in our bodies longer than the other brain chemicals, triggered by failure, chastisement, shame from others, and stewing on a problem ourselves, which can suppress the immune system, increase blood pressure, and decrease libido.

If you are feeling the negative effects of Cortisol, simply flush your mind with positive beliefs including: 'Pain is a signal to grow, not to suffer. Once we learn the lesson the pain is teaching us, the pain goes away. In life, there are no mistakes, only lessons. Remember, failure is an event, not a person. There is a difference between the person and the performance. We never lose, if we always learn. Nothing happens to us, everything happens For us, to give us experience, for our personal development, and for good.

For leaders and coaches, this means that discipline is to teach, not to punish. You can't increase a person's performance by making him feel worse. Humiliation immobilizes our behavior!

Remember, the most effective and admired leaders and speakers only tell stories that trigger the Five Positive Brain Chemicals!

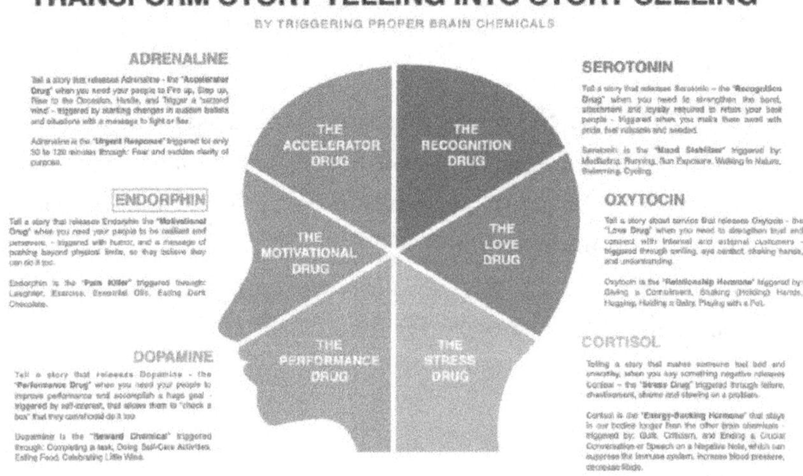

Using Brain Chemicals to Turn Story Telling into Story Selling

Once we fully understand the art and science of storytelling, our natural progression takes us to the up-leveled mindset and heart-set we call 'Story Selling.' Why? People don't buy what we sell. They buy what we believe. They buy our story. They buy into our culture - especially when we are the ones challenging the status quo, which attracts them to want to be part of our 'tribe.'

Some call these unique individuals 'hell-raisers,' and some call them revolutionaries. Yet, they become some of the most powerful, influential, effective, admired, successful, and significant leaders in every industry, in every generation. Why?

They challenge thoughts, and processes, and disrupt the status quo. They push. They raise the bar for everyone else and they call people out. They see things differently. They know no one wants to be sold features and benefits, but everybody wants to buy into an exciting lifestyle and work-style movement.

But they are renegades living and thinking 'outside the fire,' so how do they generate interest and loyalty in their philosophies, ideals, products, services, and clear causes? They tell a passionate story that reveals their purpose and attracts those who believe what they believe, which triggers one of the Brain Chemicals to buy into their entire value proposition.

Thomas Edison didn't sell a light bulb. He sold the romantic story of sitting with family and friends in a lighted home. The Wright Brothers didn't sell an airplane. They sold the storied dream of traveling faster to wonderful destinations that would shrink the world. Henry Ford didn't sell automobiles. He sold the story of prestigious, affordable travel for everybody. Steven Jobs didn't sell computers. He sold the story of being part of a complete lifestyle makeover and joining the hippest, coolest, most innovative movement in online connection and music enjoyment.

Steven Jobs quantified this 'cult of personality' in his 1997 television commercial by honoring the maverick souls who use their stories to sell:

> "Here's to the crazy ones, the misfits, the rebels, the ones
> who see things differently. You can quote them, disagree with
> them, glorify or vilify them, but you can't ignore them.
> Because the ones who are crazy enough to think they can
> change the world are the ones who do."

Chapter Five

Turning Story Telling
into Story Selling

A Deeper Dive into the Brain Chemicals

Adrenaline

"85% of our financial success is due to our personality and ability to communicate. Shockingly, only 15% is due to knowledge and technical skill." – Dale Carnegie

As we pointed out in Chapter Two, storytelling is quite the buzzword right now. However, it seems most chatter about storytelling only focuses on how to talk about your product to consumers. I want to go a step further and focus on how storytelling can be applied to our process of creating products.

I know that if a lot of people were to approach their colleagues or bosses about applying tactics from storytelling to the product development process, they wouldn't get a lot of support. Many people dismiss the idea of storytelling. But the truth is, there is real science that supports the power of stories.

In his book 'Start With Why', my friend and colleague Simon Sinek's theory on Story Selling is that successfully communicating the passion behind the 'Why' is a way to communicate with the listener's limbic brain - the part of the listener's brain that influences behavior. Sinek says, "Starting with Why makes Apple more than just a computer company selling features and benefits, and that's why their products have flourished while their competitors' products with similar technology and capabilities have often flopped."

Think about a time when someone told you a story that you just couldn't stop thinking about - a movie or a book. Why is it that we remember those so well? It turns out that the secret lies in how our brain processes fact or fiction.

In a 2012 New York Times article, called Your Brain on Fiction, author Annie Murphy Paul examines how stories affect our brains and also our actions in real life. In the article, she writes:

"A well-written or well-told story goes beyond simulating reality to give readers and listeners an experience unavailable off the page and stage: to enter fully into other people's thoughts and feelings."

But how does this happen? When your brain is exposed to information and facts, two parts of your brain are activated: Broca's area and Wernicke's area. These two areas of the brain are responsible for turning words into meaning.

A well-told story, with many intricate details, will cause your brain to light up and engage. For example, if the narrative has descriptors related to smell, the brain's olfactory cortex is engaged. And if the narrative includes movement, the motor cortex is activated.

Don't Retell a Story – Relive It!

Therefore, when we are reading or hearing a story, it often feels like we're really in it – we visualize the location, and the people, we hear their voices, smell scents, taste food, and feel touch and emotion. This isn't just our imagination. This is the impact of our brain responding to the fiction.

Research shows that our brains can't tell the difference between whether we are reading or hearing about something or if we've experienced it. When all parts of our brain are engaged, an experience is created - and we recall experiences and stories better than facts.

So, if a story creates a memorable experience in the minds of collaborators, isn't it time to apply storytelling principles to your product development process and sales presentations to make it 'Story-Selling?'

Five Positive Brain Chemicals

The brain manufactures and releases a total of Six Chemicals. Cortisol is harmful and remains in our bodies longer than the other chemicals creating a debilitating effect on our health and performance. This leaves Five Positive Brain Chemicals that enhance our ability to fire up, quickly connect, create trust, influence thinking and behavior, and close more deals:

Adrenaline

Commonly known as the "fight or flight" hormone, Adrenaline is produced by the adrenal glands after receiving a sudden and startling message from the brain that a stressful situation has presented itself. The primary role of Adrenaline is arousal. When you are stressed, you become more aware, awake, focused, and generally more responsive. Adrenaline increases heart rate, which helps to shift blood flow away from areas where it might not be so crucial, like the skin, and toward more essential areas at the time, like the muscles, so with a surge of energy, you can flee the stressful scene.

A man is four hours from home on a road trip and injures his knee playing basketball with his associates. He heard a pop; it swelled up into a huge black and blue ball, and his colleagues carried him to his hotel room. An hour later, his buddies phone him and invite him to join them for Happy Hour in the lobby sports bar. He is lying in bed with ice on his propped-up, throbbing leg, and declines, complaining, 'I'm in so much pain. I know I tore something and will need surgery. I'm worried about how I'm going to work and pay my bills. I can't walk and dread the thought of trying to bend my leg enough to get in a car. It's my right leg so I can't drive, and I will need some help getting home tomorrow! Sorry, but I can't move because of the excruciating pain!'

But… as soon as he hangs up the phone it rings again. This time the voice asks, 'Is this John Doe? My name is Bob Dunne, I am a police officer. Your wife has just been in a serious automobile accident, and she is in critical condition. My advice is that you better hustle to the hospital as fast as you can, or you might not see her alive.'

Suddenly his knee doesn't hurt anymore. Suddenly, he has energy and can walk (hobble) and bend his swollen leg, and he calls his colleague back to see if he will drive him to the hospital to his beloved wife's side.

This is Adrenaline – triggered by urgency, worry, devotion, hope, faith, and focus on leaving no regrets!

The story continues: as they get in his car and race away, his phone rings again. It is the same officer who now apologizes and confesses, 'Is this John Doe? I have made a horrible mistake and gave you incorrect information. Your wife was not in an accident and is healthy and fine at your home. Sorry to alarm you.'

Suddenly he gets another shot of Adrenaline – this time triggered by anger, disgust, and relief.

This same scenario occurs in sports when the score in the game suddenly is tied, and all the players on both teams get a shot of adrenaline. By raising their voices in a do-or-die, now or never excitement, the coaches trigger another shot of adrenaline that literally 'fires up' the players to tap into their 'second wind' and extra effort hustle.

In the documentary, **'The Last Dance,'** we learn how and why Michael Jordan was able to trigger adrenaline whenever he needed it to level up his performance. Charles Barkley explains that he, Michael Jordan, and Team USA Coach Chuck Daly played 18 holes of golf on the morning of a game against Puerto Rico. Barkley and Coach left, but Michael stayed to play another 18 holes. In the locker room before the game, Barkley and the Coach thought Jordan would surely be too exhausted to play at his best, but Michael told Coach he wanted to guard their star player who had trash-talked him in the media.

Jordan finished the game with 42 points, 12 rebounds, 6 steals, and held his opponent to only 6 points in a humiliating performance! The player's derogatory words ignited in Jordan a personal vendetta to teach him a lesson, which triggered adrenaline, giving Jordan extreme focus and extra energy to intensify his play! Basketball Alert! If you are competing against Michael Jordan, Don't Tick Him Off!

Story: "The Afghan Battle of Perseverance"

On the cold morning of April 6, 2008, Captain Kyle Walton was tasked with the dangerous mission of taking his elite team of warriors into the remote Shok Valley, Afghanistan – a terrorist stronghold of the notorious HIG militant group. At the crack of dawn, this 12-man U.S. Special Forces team (often called the Green Berets), and 20 U.S. trained Afghan commandos, each carrying 60 to 80 pounds of gear, were lowered out of helicopters onto sharp, ice-covered rocks and into freezing water at an altitude of 10,000 feet.

As they made their way up the steep mountain terrain toward a cluster of thick-walled mud buildings, the insurgents scrambled to their fighting positions and for the next seven hours, unloaded a barrage of machine gun, sniper fire and rocket-propelled grenades onto the exposed soldiers - shooting at each of the U.S. positions from virtually all sides. As countless bullets ricocheted off the rocks, two rounds slammed into Walton's helmet, smashing his head into the ground.

Immediately an Afghan interpreter was killed. Staff Sergeant Luis Morales was shot in the right thigh and Staff Sergeant Dillon Behr was hit in the hip. Morales and Walton pulled Behr back to their position where Morales cut open Behr's fatigues and applied pressure to his bleeding wound. Moments later, Morales was hit again, in the ankle, leaving him struggling to treat himself and his comrade.

Suddenly Staff Sergeant John Wayne Walding was hit below his right knee and saw that the bullet amputated his right leg. What would you have done? Walding grabbed his boot and put it in his crotch, then got the boot laces and tied it to his thigh, so it would not flop around while he continued to shoot at the bad guys and help his brothers win the fight.

A round suddenly hit Staff Sgt. Ford in the chest, knocking him back but not penetrating his body armor. A minute later, another bullet went through his left arm and shoulder, hitting the helmet of the medic, Staff Sgt. Ronald J. Shurer, who was behind him treating Behr.

Bleeding heavily from the arm, Ford coordinated with Air Force Joint Tactical Air Controller (JTAC) Zachary Rhyner to radio in Air Force jets to begin dropping bombs on enemy positions until they walked and carried the wounded to the streambed.

A medivac helicopter flew in, but because of the relentless barrage of bullets coming from the enemy, the pilot hovered just long enough for the medic to jump off and then flew away. Another helicopter came in but was forced down in the middle of the fast-moving river, where it took two or three men to carry each of the wounded to safety. As they took off under heavy fire, a bullet grazed the pilot's head.

At battle's end, two Afghan Commandos were killed, and the Green Berets had suffered fifteen wounded, while an estimated two hundred insurgents were dead.

For their bravery and perseverance under fire, Walton and his men (10 total) received the Silver Star Medal - the third-highest military decoration awarded for valor and gallantry in action.

In 2018, Ronald Shurer's, and Matthew O. Williams's Silver Stars were upgraded to the military's highest honor: the Congressional Medal of Honor. Zachary Rhyner was awarded the Air Force Cross.

When asked why and how they were able to overcome the massive odds and live to fight another day, Walding said, "We obeyed our instincts and Special Forces Creed, which allowed us to trust our training and fight for each other as a true band of brothers!"

Chapter Six

The Power of Emotional Response

A Deeper Dive into Endorphin and Dopamine

Endorphin

Endorphin is the "motivational drug" and "natural high" that masks physical pain. We humans are inherently built for endurance and don't give up because we are tired. We persist because it also feels good. That's why we love to exercise. For a speaker, Endorphins are triggered in our listeners in two ways: with laugh-out-loud humor, and when we share a "Rocky" type inspirational story of someone who has pushed him/herself beyond their physical limits, reaffirming that 'when your attitude is right, your abilities will always catch up!'

For these reasons, the ultimate sales presentation takes our potential buyers on an emotional roller coaster ride that gives them a periodic shot of Endorphins as they laugh, think, and cry, believing they can also fight through obstacles if they believe and confidently act on those beliefs!

Story: "George Washington – Divinely Called"

When any of us question if America's Founding Fathers, authors of the Constitution, and framers of freedom were divinely guided and inspired, let us reflect on the true story of our 'Bulletproof President.'

As a young man, George Washington was the 'courier' for the British Commander General Braddock in the French and Indian War. Braddock was mortally wounded in a battle in 1755, and all the other couriers were killed. By the end of the war, Washington had had two horses shot out from beneath him, had four bullet holes in his jacket and bullet fragments in his hair, but no flesh wounds.

Many years later, before Washington became President, one of the Indian Chiefs who had fought in the war asked his braves to take him to meet Washington. When he shook Washington's hand, he proclaimed, 'I am an expert marksman and shot you seventeen times, and my warriors shot you, and I eventually told them to stop wasting their bullets on you! I am elderly, and before I die, I needed to meet the man who was protected by the Great Presence Above!'

Regardless of your political bias, certain leaders in American history, including George Washington and Abraham Lincoln, have been 'called' and protected by God to lead and preserve our nation. It is no surprise why we have 'In God We Trust' on our money and swear in our government leaders with their hand on the Bible.

What you are feeling is Endorphin reminding you of the Divine Intervention in the establishment of freedom.

Joke: "Defend Your Honor"

A man was sitting at a table in the bar. Suddenly, two huge men came in the door, walked up to him, and beat the ever-living tar out of him. Leaving him unconscious and in a pool of blood on the floor, the two men strutted out of the bar. As they left, they stopped the bartender and proudly said, "When he wakes up, tell him that was Karate from Korea and Judo from Japan!"

In a few minutes, the guy came to, stood up, wiped himself off, finished his drink, and left.

Ten minutes later, the two men came back to the bar. While they were drinking and laughing, the guy they beat up came back into the bar, walked straight up to their table, and knocked both of them out cold. As he left, he told the bartender, "When they wake up, tell them that was a crowbar from Sears!"

Message Joke: "The Homeless Preacher"

One Sunday morning, a man who was homeless dressed in ragged, smelly clothes, carrying a worn-out Bible, entered an upscale, wealthy church in an exclusive neighborhood. As the man took a seat, those near him moved away, protected their children in disgust, and held their noses. When the preacher finished 'saving souls' he approached him and explained that in a posh church like his, there is a dress code and suggested that he ask God what he should wear before he came back.

The next Sunday, the same homeless man showed up again wearing the same torn, filthy clothes and once again took a seat. The pompous parishioners again shunned and ignored him. When the preacher saw him, he bee-lined straight to his bench and scolded, 'I thought I told you to ask God what the proper attire is for worshiping in a wealthy church like mine.'

'I did,' he replied, 'and God told me that He didn't know what I should wear in your church because He's never been here before!'

Story: "Pressure Creates Peak Performance"

Two of the greatest single examples of the power of Endorphins were illuminated during the 1988 World Series and the 2024 World Series.

In 1988, the Oakland A's were favored to beat the Los Angeles Dodgers. It was game one at Dodger Stadium and very few experts gave LA a chance to win because their MVP superstar slugger Kirk Gibson could barely walk due to two swollen knees and a nagging hamstring injury. He wasn't even introduced before the game. Too hurt to play, Gibson reluctantly stayed in the locker room receiving physical therapy and treatment while watching the game on TV.

Suddenly the phone on the wall rang and Manager Tommy Lasorda asked Kirk to come up to the field to pinch-hit in the bottom of the ninth inning. The Dodgers were behind 4-3, teammate Mike Davis was on first base, and with two outs, Gibson limped onto the field to ignite Dodger fans into a crazed frenzy!

Hall of Fame A's pitcher Dennis Eckersley was the intimidating closer who had allowed only five home runs all year. Gibson came out swinging, hitting four fouls, taking three balls, and facing a Full-Count.

Kirk turned on the next fastball and using only his arms, miraculously hit the game-winning home run! With the fans screaming, he threw his arm in the air, hobbled around the bases, and was mobbed as he touched home base! Game over! Oakland could never recover, and the Dodgers went on to win this World Series 4 games to 1.

Story: "2024 World Series"

In the 2024 World Series, Game 1, 10th inning with the Yankees ahead of the Dodgers 3-2, Dodgers Freddie Freeman hobbles to the plate nursing a serious ankle injury. With two outs and bases loaded, he hits a grand slam to win the game! In Game 2, he launched a solo home run to help win the game. In both Games 3 and 4, he blasted two-run homers. In Game 5, trailing the Yankees in the fifth inning 5-0, Freeman hit a double, which ignited a 5-run rally to tie the score, and win the game to be crowned World Champions! Freeman was named MVP, with 4 home runs and 12 RBIs!

Dopamine

Dopamine is the "accomplishment/performance drug" that's triggered both when we feel like we are making progress, and when we achieve our goal – during the journey - and when we arrive at our previously decided upon destination. For a Sales Professional, when we tell a story about overcoming obstacles and persevering against all odds that ends in triumph over tragedy, we give our prospect a shot of Dopamine.

When we share a story that allows our potential customers to "check a box", that they have also done it, or could do it, they feel Dopamine.

Both Endorphins and Dopamine are triggered when we share a compelling vision and detail how cool it will be when they achieve the amazing accomplishment. For this reason, Endorphins and Dopamine are the "selfish chemicals" triggered by self-interest. They are very addictive because the feelings don't last, and everybody wants the exhilarating feeling again.

Story: "Leave No Regrets"

Ronald Wayne was 25 years old, working with Steve Jobs at Atari before he, Jobs, and Wozniak founded Apple Computer on April 1, 1976. Serving as the venture's "adult supervisor," Wayne drew the first Apple Logo, wrote the three men's original Partnership Agreement, and wrote the operating Owner's Manual for the new Apple 1 computer.

In the Agreement Wayne received a 10% stake in Apple, but because all members of a partnership are personally responsible for any debts incurred by any partner; and because Wayne was still licking his wounds from a failed company that he had started five years earlier, on April 12, less than two weeks later, Wayne sold his equity interest back to Jobs and Wozniak for $800.

Apple immediately started attracting investors and was turned into a corporation, where one year after leaving Apple, Wayne received $1,500 for his agreement to forfeit any claims against the new company.

In its first year of operations (1976), Apple's sales reached $174,000. With sustained growth, in 2019, Apple became the first company of its kind to reach a market valuation of one trillion dollars U.S. Had Ronald Wayne kept his 10% stock and 'persevered' until then, it would now be worth over 60 billion dollars!

What you are now feeling is dopamine because you are telling yourself, 'I am in the process of making my dream come true, so I will never quit, calculate my risks, and Leave No Regrets!'

Story: "Never Say Never!"

During a weekend in January 2022, all four NFL Divisional Playoff games were won on last-second plays! The 49ers had rebounded from a

3-5 start with 5 losses in 6 games and defeated the Packers on a last-second field goal. The kicker had just missed a previous kick!

With 15 seconds left in the game, Bengals Quarterback Joe Burrows threw a 19-yard pass that set up the winning field goal to beat the Titans!

The Rams were beating Tampa Bay 27-3. But in his classic 'never-say-never' mindset, 44-year-old quarterback Tom Brady rallied his Buccaneers back to tie the game 27-27. But with 42 seconds left in the game, Rams QB Matt Stafford drove his team down for the kicker (who had previously missed) to win the game 30-27.

In the final thriller, Kansas City and Buffalo collectively scored 25 points in the last 2 minutes of the game. With 13 seconds remaining, Bills quarterback Josh Allen threw a go-ahead touchdown pass. But Chief's quarterback Patrick Mahomes refused to lose and threw two passes to march the Chiefs 44 yards to set up Butker's 49-yard field goal to tie the game. He had already missed twice. The Chiefs won in overtime. Mahomes was asked what he said in the huddle and replied, "I told my guys I loved them and that we've been dreaming about this moment since we were kids. This is our time, so let's go finish this thing" - giving his teammates a shot of adrenaline, endorphins, and dopamine, which they responded to with renewed focus and energy to win!

Story: "Performance Enhancing Drugs!"

In the 2024 Summer Olympic Games, Team USA was playing a must-win semi-final game against Serbia and their two NBA superstars: 3-time MVP Nikola Jokić and shooting sensation Bogdan Bogdanovic.

Serbia was ahead of the U.S. for 35:12 minutes, nearly 90% of the game. But because Team USA triggered in each other adrenaline, endorphins, and dopamine, they were able to out-hustle and out-score the Serbs by 17 points in 12 minutes to win at the buzzer 95-91.

Because Steph Curry was filled with these brain chemicals, he was able to take over the game with 36 points, with nine 3-pointers, making the last four 'mind-blowing' 3-pointers to win the game! When Team USA celebrated, they also got a shot of Serotonin and Oxytocin!

Chapter Seven

The Power of Influence and Persuasion

A Deeper Dive into Serotonin

The 'Addictive' Drugs

As we continue with our discussion, let me point out that Adrenaline, Endorphins, and Dopamine are highly addictive drugs, which are critical in the process of transforming Storytelling into Story Selling. Why?

The purpose of a leader is to grow more leaders who believe what you believe, not generate more followers (with stories)!

The goal is not to do business with everybody who wants what you have. The goal is to do business only with those who believe what you believe, so they choose you, not just somebody who does what you do!

People choose us, not because of what we say, but because of how we make them feel. When we trigger Adrenaline, Endorphins, and Dopamine, the euphoric feelings are short-lived and highly addictive. Because people attach their feelings to the person who created them, they choose to engage with us, so they can feel them again!

Although not addictive, the final two brain chemicals also create distinct thoughts and feelings that influence behavior!

Serotonin

Serotonin is the "recognition drug" that is triggered when a sales professional creates feelings of gratitude and humility that immediately invite our potential customers to want to listen and learn from us. When we are thanked, it makes us feel valued. Email doesn't work - it must be in person. PowerPoint slides don't work – it must be a well-told story that makes our potential customers swell with pride and feel valuable and needed.

When we trigger Serotonin, it immediately strengthens the bond, attachment, and loyalty between a sales professional and potential buyer, leader and follower, coach and player, teacher and student.

While Dopamine is triggered when we do something, Serotonin is triggered when others find out about it and celebrate our achievement. For this reason, Sales Professionals must 'seek to bless, not impress,' proving true that people don't care how much we know until they know how much we care.

Story: "Question the Answers"

A college professor asked his students to list what they thought were the Seven Wonders of the World. Out of the hundred students in the lecture hall, the consensus was: Egypt's Pyramids, City of Petra, the Great Wall of China, Stonehenge, Taj Mahal, St. Peter's Basilica, and Machu Picchu.

While gathering the votes, the professor noted that one girl had not yet finished her paper. He asked if she was having trouble answering the question. She replied, "No, I'm not having trouble with the answer, I'm having trouble with the question.

Why only seven? According to whom and what criteria? What does 'wonder' mean to you, and is it different for me?"

The professor responded, "Tell us what you have, and maybe we can help."

The girl hesitated and then read, "I think the real Seven Wonders of the World are: to see, to hear, to taste, to touch, to laugh, to feel, and to love."

The room went quiet, and the professor whispered, "Wow! And the lesson learned? The most important and precious things in life cannot be bought or built by hand; Before we look for answers outside of ourselves, let us first look within; Life is not about answers; it's about questions.

Story: "Undying Romance and Love"

Jim Golay, from Casper, Wyoming, was diagnosed with an inoperable brain tumor and knew he wasn't going to be around for much longer. Therefore, he wanted to make Valentine's Day extra special for his wife. Unfortunately, Jim died in November.

Three months later, on February 14 of the next year, a bouquet of flowers was delivered to his home.

His wife opened the card and read, 'My beloved Shelley. I love you with all my heart, always have, always will. I miss you and can't wait to hold you again in my arms! I'm your guardian angel and close by whenever you need me! Happy Valentine's Day Babe! Love Jim.'

Confused because the note was in Jim's handwriting and angry at whoever thought this was funny, Shelley phoned the florist to find out what was going on. The florist explained that before her husband died, Jim hatched a plan to send his beloved Shelley a bouquet of her favorite flowers on Valentine's Day to remind her of his undying love!

Shelley cried tears of joy as this was the most romantic thing she had ever experienced!

A year passed, and to her surprise, a Valentine's Day bouquet and handwritten note were again delivered. Unbeknownst to Shelley, Jim had written and left enough personal notes that the florist was able to deliver one every year for the next 20 years until Shelley passed away!

Story: "Light the Fire Within"

I am always inspired by the Olympic Games and emotionally moved by the opening ceremonies. The spirit of the 2002 Winter Games in Salt Lake City especially touched my heart when they brought in the ripped, battered, and torn American flag that was flying on the World Trade Center on September 11. There wasn't a dry eye in the 50,000-seat stadium.

On February 6, the day before the Opening Ceremonies, I was deeply honored and privileged to be one of the torchbearers who carried the Olympic flame. There were only 11,520 of us who were nominated to participate in the Torch Relay, passing it from one to another over 13,500 miles through 46 states on a journey that took a total of 65 days.

I was honored to run the torch on day 63 and was blessed to be the final runner of the day, which meant I got to carry it twice as far as any other runner (1/2 mile) and light the cauldron to be transported to the beginning point for tomorrow's triumphant entry into the stadium.

That morning in our special orientation, it was pointed out with extreme emphasis that when we had our torch ignited by the oncoming torchbearer and his or her torch was immediately extinguished, each of us, for that one moment in time, would be the keeper of the sacred Olympic flame and the only one in the entire world holding and displaying the last pure sign of international world peace!

The orientation was conducted by a young man and young woman in charge of the entire sixty-five-day torch relay. Their job was to make sure every runner showed up at his or her location, so the relay never missed a beat. If there was a last-minute cancellation, they were equipped in the official van with extra running suits in every size to accommodate a last-minute replacement runner.

One morning in Houston, Texas, a call came in that an elderly woman would not be able to make it for her relay segment. Scrambling to find a qualified substitute, the young woman in charge was driving the van down the route and passed by an elementary school. She immediately stopped and ran into the building. Frantically, she introduced herself and asked the principal to help her select someone to carry the Torch. A teacher, a counselor, an A student?

No. The young woman explained, "I need a child in your school who kids make fun of, who doesn't have a lot of friends and usually sits alone - who has a tough home life and struggles with his or her schoolwork."

The principal smiled and introduced her to a tiny, shoddy-looking nine-year-old boy in the fourth grade. He was secretly outfitted in his very own official Torch Relay tracksuit, given a brief orientation, and secretly escorted out of school to join the other relay runners in the van. The students were excused from class and assembled on the side of the street in front of their school to join the thousands of people already gathered to cheer on the torchbearers who would run in front of them.

The relay van finally pulled up and stopped. The oncoming torch runner was greeted with screams and yells. As he drew near, the van door opened, and out into the street stepped the young fourth grader, all decked out in his white suit and holding the torch that was almost as big as he was. The torch bearer ignited his torch, and he began to jog.

At first sight, fellow students and school faculty members gasped in disbelief, "How did he get out there? He must have stolen the torch!"

As he ran, a schoolmate shouted out his name in disgust. But the mean comment ignited the crowd, and they started chanting his name: 'Bill-y, Bill-y!' The teachers and students couldn't believe it but were caught up in the excitement and, one by one, joined the crowd to cheer louder and louder: 'BILL-Y, BILL-Y!'

Two days later, the young woman in charge of the relay received a handwritten letter from the principal. It simply read, "You already know the power of the flame. But you have no idea what that one magical torch-running moment did to change the attitudes of my faculty and transform the tolerance level of my students. This one experience truly did 'Light the Fire Within.' Thank you. You have changed our school and our community forever. P.S. Billy no longer sits alone!"

Chapter Eight

The Power of Trust and Connection

A Deeper Dive into Oxytocin

Oxytocin

Oxytocin is the "love drug" and is quickly triggered through human touch and engaging in acts of kindness. It is most easily understood when we realize the definition of sales is the "transference of trust." It's uncomfortable to be around strangers. Therefore, a Sales Professional must first be "ordinary" and relatable before we can be "extraordinary." When we tell a story about unconditional love, spending time with friends, volunteering, and giving service to others, it immediately creates a safe and trusting environment.

When our potential customers know they can openly express their feelings, show emotion, and actively participate in our presentation, they get a shot of Oxytocin, which is the drug that makes us want to buy products and services, and volunteer our time or give our resources to a worthy cause.

Human Touch. Therefore, Significant Sales Professionals seek to interact with potential customers before their official meeting in a social or philanthropic setting and then greet them as they enter your appointment with a warm smile, caring eye connection, and a firm and confident handshake that genuinely connects us head-to-head and trusting heart to trusting heart. Oxytocin is the catalyst in creating a legacy organization that is larger than us, making our work meaningful so our lives matter.

Oxytocin is also triggered when we call someone on the phone and especially when we visit him/her in person. Email is a good way to transfer and exchange information, but it does not trigger Oxytocin no matter what you write in the message. If someone emails or texts you a question, don't answer back in a typed response. When it is logistically possible you should go to them and create a physical, intellectual, and spiritual human connection, which triggers Oxytocin and accelerates, amplifies, and strengthens trust because they can actually see and feel that you really do care.

Volunteerism and Acts of Kindness. When we volunteer our time, donate money and/or serve someone in need, we trigger Oxytocin,

Most importantly, Oxytocin strengthens our immune system and makes us healthier, happier, and more productive. While Endorphin and Dopamine are highly addictive, Oxytocin fortifies us against becoming addicted – even blocking our vulnerability to opioid and hardcore drug addiction.

Bottom line. Every sales presentation should begin with a positive high that releases Endorphins and Dopamine, then trigger Serotonin by acknowledging what a privilege it is to serve them and how courageous they are in deciding to solve their problem and end the meeting with a call to action that gives them a shot of Oxytocin that emotionally empowers them to sign the contract and do the deal.

Story: "The Circus"

When I was a young boy, my dad and I were standing in line to buy tickets for the circus. Finally, there was only one family between us and the ticket counter. There were eight children, all probably under the age of twelve. You could tell they didn't have a lot of money. Their clothes were not expensive, and it was clear they had never been to the circus before, as they jabbered about the clowns, elephants, and what they would see that night.

The father and mother were at the head of the pack, standing proud as could be. The mother was holding her husband's hand, looking up at him as if to say, "You're my knight in shining armor." He was smiling and basking in pride, looking at her as if to reply, "You got that right."

The man asked the ticket lady, "I would like to buy eight children's tickets and two adult tickets so I can take my family to the circus."

The ticket lady quoted the price, and his wife let go of his hand. Her head dropped. The man's lip began to quiver. The father leaned a little closer and asked, "How much did you say?" The ticket lady again quoted the price.

The man didn't have enough money. How was he supposed to turn and tell his eight kids that he didn't have enough money to take them to the circus?

Seeing what was going on, and determined to help the man retain his dignity, my dad put his hand into his pocket, pulled out a twenty-dollar bill, and dropped it on the ground. He then reached down, picked up the bill, tapped the man on the shoulder, and said, "Excuse me, sir, this fell out of your pocket."

The man knew what was going on. He looked straight into my dad's eyes, took my dad's hand in both of his, squeezed tightly onto the twenty-dollar bill, and with a tear streaming down his cheek, he replied, "Thank you, sir. This means sir world to me and my family."

My dad and I went back to our car and drove home. We didn't go to the circus that night, but we didn't go without.

Story: "Earth Angel Dad"

My dad battled cancer for six-and-a-half years. When he passed away, my siblings and I gathered at my mother's home to plan the Celebration of Life. Suddenly, the phone rang, and Mom answered. The lady on the other end asked if this was Ruby Clark. Mom said, 'Yes.' She asked if her late husband was S. Wayne Clark. Nervously, Mom inquired, 'Who is this?' The lady explained she had just seen my dad's photo in the Obituary Section of our local newspaper and needed to share a story.

She said years ago, she was a young mother with a new baby, and her man had walked out on her. Desperately, she prayed and felt prompted to go to the grocery store, and a miracle would occur. Humbly, she put some diapers, baby formula, and bread in her cart and stood away from the cashier, wondering what to do. When she finally stepped up to the counter, the cashier said the man in front of her had paid for her groceries and left another $100 bill for her to fill her cart!

He had already driven away when she ran out of the store to thank him. She recognized Dad's picture in the newspaper and tracked down Mom's number to share her story and ask to attend the funeral.

The spiritual message is that Dad had never shopped at this Albertsons and was only there that day to buy a specific item that another store did not have. My dad's life of service before self proves true that when we pray, God answers our prayers through other people!

Story: "Operation Smile"

After graduating from both dental school and medical school, Dr. Bill Magee and his wife Kathy organized some doctors to travel to the Philippines to repair underserved children's cleft lips and palates.

With limited time and resources, they did all they could but had to turn away hundreds of heartbroken mothers and crying children.

Realizing the incalculable need for their services, they made a commitment to return, and Operation Smile was conceived and born that day. Word spread throughout the land, and the anticipation of the returning doctors excited those who needed their help. One man, twenty-three-year-old José, heard about these free surgeries, and although he lived in a village a three-day journey away, he felt this was his hope for a new life and set out for Manila.

José had a three-pound tumor on his chin that was so large and grotesque that his family kept him hidden from public view his entire life, forcing him to live as a prison in his own body. People believed he had this deformity because he was possessed by the devil, he was never allowed to attend school, no one would hire him to work, and he only went out at night under the guise of a bandana.

With no money for travel, José set out on his long journey, walking over a rugged mountain pass, forging a river, and trekking for countless miles along the dusty back roads until he finally arrived in Manila.

Amidst hundreds of parents and their small children, Jose was the lone adult hoping for a miracle. As the screening process got underway, José did not qualify for treatment as the priority of the mission was pediatric care. Sadly, he walked the three-day journey back home.

Six months later, the word spread that Operation Smile was returning to Manila. Thinking he would give it another chance, José again made the three-day journey only to be turned away a second time for the same reasons. Devastated, he walked back home.

On the verge of suicide, believing his life didn't matter to anyone, José heard Operation Smile was returning to Manila and decided to try his luck one last time and walk to Manila.

This time José's name was the last one called. He had passed the screening tests and would receive his surgery the next morning! As José was given his number, he started thinking about all the ways his life would immediately change. He had never kissed his mother good night. Maybe he could finally have a friend?

But as he turned to leave, José encountered a crying mother whose little girl would have been next in line for surgery except for the lack of resources. Instinctively, he gave the little girl his number, and with tears in his eyes, José slowly trekked his way back to his village.

When Dr. Magee found out, he accessed the medical information they had gathered during the screening, found José in his village, and flew him to Virginia, where Dr. Magee removed the 3-pound tumor.

I met José when we shared the program as speakers at an Operation Smile Leadership Conference, where this handsome man showed a wedding photo next to his beautiful wife, and a second photo holding their beautiful newborn baby! Yes, kindness triggers Oxytocin!

Chapter Nine

Preparation: Mindset, Technical, Performance, Content

"All the world's a stage; And all the men and women merely players; They have their exits and their entrances; And one man in his time plays many parts" – Shakespeare As You Like It

Every corporate executive, manager, leader, coach, and teacher is judged by his/her articulation, use of proper grammar, eye contact, the flawless execution of their prepared and polished plan, and non-verbal communication that projects attitude, energy, confident presence, authenticity, believability and the 'transference of trust.'

This holds true for entertainers, actors, dancers, singers, and athletes, who are held by the public to a high expectation, believing the performer's communication skills should mirror and match the same level of physical performance they witness on stage or in athletic competition.

This applies to public speaking and performance of every kind, highlighting the significance of attitude and energy. Attitude is conveyed through posture, shoulders back, head high, with a smile that collectively is referred to as the 'magic eye' that must be projected from the stage to the attendees sitting on the very last row in the venue.

Energy is controlled and projected by interpersonal communication that shifts perspective. If you are nervous and afraid before you perform, it means you think it's about you – your ego believes the audience members are there for you. But if you are excited before you perform, it means it's about them – you are there for the audience to show off your extreme preparation. It's the exact same chemical reaction in your brain, but one perspective triggers negative energy, causing stress, anxiety, tightening muscles, perspiration, and debilitating cortisol. The other perspective triggers positive energy, filling a relaxed body with endorphin, dopamine, serotonin, and oxytocin that increases blood flow, concentration, and focused peak performance!

However, maximizing the effect of these brain chemicals also requires what mindset coach Dave Austin calls getting 'Game Ready.'

Story: "Game Ready – Artist in the Mirror"

When silver is heated up, because each vat of the molten metal responds differently to the same temperature, the artist has but one technique to know when the liquid stands ready for pouring into a beautiful shape. Only when the artist can see their face reflecting back at them from the silver, is it ready to be molded into a masterpiece.

Whenever we feel the heat during a test of what we are made of, we must look at the artist in the mirror reflecting back at us to know when we are ready to mold and shape who we are into the 'something more' that we have the potential to become.

Story: "Derek Hough"

When I helped my friend Derek Hough: 6-time winner of the coveted Dancing With The Stars 'Mirror Ball Trophy' and celebrity Judge, write his speech & focus on his book, he taught me that contestants are judged on three elements:

- Technicality – the finely tuned skills that allow us to execute the movement at the highest level of proficiency.

- Performance – the passionate connection we have with the audience that makes our polished skills come alive!

- Content – the choreography that showcases if we are taking the easy road of complacency or pushing ourselves beyond our past best personal performance.

Would you win the Dance of Life if you were judged on your skills, authenticity & ambition?

Derek takes pride in knowing he is always judged in every aspect of his life by this same criterion and doesn't look at it as 'pressure.' He looks at it as a continuous challenge for him to live his life to the fullest, which naturally makes him a positive role model.

FYI – besides being one of the very best professional dancers in the world – a world champion Latin and Ballroom Dancer way before we saw him on DWTS – Derek is a choreographer, actor, singer and became a judge on the series and a judge on another competition show called The World of Dance!

The most significant compliment I can pay Derek is that he is exactly and always the same on & off stage. Are you? This is why we always listen when Derek speaks, and especially when he tells a story. His life story is in perfect alignment with every performance we see on stage, so we believe him, and leave inspired to do our best to be like him!

Story: "Donny Osmond"

What would happen if you out-dreamed, out-smiled, out-worked your competition?

When I helped my friend Donny Osmond write his keynote speech for the RootsTech Conference, we had to figure out how to answer the #1 question on everyone's mind: Why is Donny Osmond speaking at a conference on Family History and genealogy? He is an entertainer! He sings Puppy Love, Go Away Little Girl, Soldier of Love, and Who!

To introduce Donny, they showed a video montage of his entire career that began when he was a little boy singing on the Andy Williams TV show, that showed his illustrious career meeting Elvis and performing with Bob Hope, Cher, Lucille Ball, and every other huge name you can think of – including performing for the Queen of England. Wow is an understatement.

When the video concluded and the applause stopped, Donny said, 'My life has been documented since I was five years old. Has Yours? If not, why not? My life is not more important you're your life – my stories are not more important than your stories - especially to your brothers and sisters, children, grandchildren, friends, coworkers, and neighbors. The life lessons I've learned from my experiences are not more important or profound than the life lessons you've learned and should be teaching your loved ones and the world!'

Donny continued, 'This is why it is an honor for me to be here today to share some stories about my ancestors that illuminate why I look the way I do, why my DNA dictated that I was born to be a singer and some of the crazy experiences I've had that have brought me to this stage.'

All 10,000 attendees in the convention center arena were now mesmerized and craving to hear Donny's stories!

As my five-hour interview continued with Donny, I learned his career began at age 5, with 33 gold records, 62 albums selling 100 million copies, hosting the Donny and Marie Show from 1976-79, performing 2000 shows of Joseph Amazing Technicolor Dreamcoat, starring on Broadway, winning Dancing With The Stars, starring with his sister Marie in a Las Vegas Strip Headlining 'Residency' Show from 2008-19 and continuing with his own solo show from 2021 and beyond! Why?

Because Donny has remained true to Donny for sixty years: family-centered, physically fit (handsome), mentally tough, spiritually strong, emotionally sound, and always bringing his A-Game to every performance! I've seen Donny perform live over 20 times, and he always gives it everything he's got – with energy, charisma, humility, class, and sophisticated elegance enough to make every person in the backstage 'meet and greet' feel they were the most important fan he had!

Longevity in anything comes when we focus on these same priorities that never change! And in each of these priorities, we create stories and learn lessons that are worth sharing with the world!

Story: "Garth Brooks"

Do You Live What You Sing?

In 1990 I was not a fan of Country Music. Garth Brooks was a new artist and I had not heard his music. Yet I was the keynote entertainer who opened for Garth at the Texas State Fair that October. The night before I had a call from my buddy Cliff Dugosh, a student body leader at Texas A&M University (where I had spoken before) who congratulated me on this awesome gig and then asked about my sick father. When I told him he had just died on October 12, Cliff jumped in his truck and drove 2 hours to meet me in the hotel parking lot just to play me a Garth Brooks song that put my dad's battle with cancer in perspective: *I could have missed the pain, But I'd have had to miss the dance* After three replays and crying together I returned to my hotel room and turned on the TV to break the silence. Wouldn't you know it? The TV was turned to CMA Country Music Television and the music video of this amazing song 'The Dance' started playing. I watched and cried some more and couldn't wait to meet Garth the next evening!

A few years later when I again shared the program with Garth, I told him this story and he dedicated The Dance to my dad in the show!

Now *I Thank God for Unanswered Prayers* and publicly acknowledge *I have Friends In Low Places & I'm Too Young To Be This Damn Old*, asking: *Is the love I gave her in the past, Gonna be enough to last, If tomorrow never comes?*

Are people inspired by what you say and do? By what criterion is your life being judged? As a storyteller, will people believe you and be inspired by you because you are the same off-stage as you are on stage? Are your stories an actual reflection of not just what you know, but who you are, and what you live? Are you winning the Dance of Life, the Performance of Life, and Singing the Song of Life?

Story: "Shun Fujimoto"

Is your current 'Mindset' merely positive or is it an unstoppable Mental Toughness? Mindset is the story you believe about yourself. Mental Toughness is how you respond to your story. Your Mental Toughness is increased, strengthened, and sustained when your 'why' and reason for rising to the occasion is bigger and more meaningful than your 'why-not.' When your story includes 'I can, I will,' you can even outperform your physical fitness, and over-ride and over-compensate for physical pain.

Going into the 1976 Olympic Summer Games in Montreal, Canada, the Japanese Men's Gymnastics team had dominated the world, winning four consecutive Team Gold Medals in the previous four Olympic Games. However, it was Shun Fujimoto who helped his country win the Fifth Gold by competing on a broken leg in two further events.

Fujimoto knew that in such a tight contest there was no way the Japanese team could win the Gold if he did not compete.

After sustaining his excruciating injury during his floor exercise, Shun moved to his pommel horse routine, scoring 9.5. When he dismounted, he fought through the debilitating pain and moved on to the final event, the rings, fighting not to limp.

He knew that even if he could make it through this last performance he would have to land on his injured leg and stand tall and steady-straight for three full seconds after a complicated spinning dismount from a height of almost three meters. He also knew he had to score at least 9.5 out of 10 for his team to win!

Not only did Shun complete the routine, but he delivered the best performance of his entire career, made a solid landing on both feet and remained standing, to record an incredible 9.7, despite dislocating his kneecap and tearing the ligaments in his broken leg in the process.

In the film footage of his Olympic competition, as Fujimoto lands his routine, not only can you see what happens to his leg, but you can see Shun trying not to let the pain show.

Because of his heroic performance, Japan's team defeated the Soviets by four-tenths of a point to win the Gold Medal for the fifth straight Olympic Games in a row!

Story: "Spartacus"

An all-encompassing illustration that illuminates everything this chapter is about is the famous story of *Spartacus*. Spartacus, a historically based movie about a gladiator who led an uprising of slaves against the Roman legions in 71 B.C., features an incredibly powerful scene.

Spartacus (played by Kirk Douglas) and his slave army had defeated the Romans twice until General Marcus Crassus finally defeated them. Crassus tells the thousand captured soldiers: 'You will die by crucifixion unless you point out to us Spartacus, for we do not know him by sight.

Spartacus immediately stands up and says, 'I am Spartacus.' The man next to him also quickly stands and says, 'No, I am Spartacus.' Another man stands and then another and another until within a minute all thousand men are standing, proclaiming, 'I am Spartacus!' Each man, by standing up, chose death.

But the loyalty of Spartacus's army was not for Spartacus. Their loyalty was to a shared vision and common cause that Spartacus inspired - the possibility that they could be free men. This cause was so intoxicating that not even one of the slaves could bear to give up on it and return to captivity. Are you standing in your truth in a powerful enough way to be someone's 'Spartacus' when they need you?

Chapter Ten

Finding Your Own Stories

"Everyone tells a story about themselves inside their own head. Always. All the time. That story makes you who you are. We either build ourselves out of that story or tear ourselves down. Stories can cause fear or conquer it. They can make the heart bigger or smaller — our sense of self-worth strong or weak. Change your story in your mind, change your life. If you do not tell the truth about yourself, you cannot tell it about other people." – Patrick Rothfuss

Whenever I conduct my Speaker Bootcamps and Master Classes, the number one comment and question from participants is: Your stories are so amazing Dan. I don't have incredible stories like yours. Nothing exciting ever happens to me. I have not had incredible adventures like you, so where am I going to find my material?

My answer is always: Stop. You are wrong! Everybody has stories and they are every bit as meaningful as mine! All you have to do is uncover them, recall them, reminisce on your experiences, and start recording them and writing them down. Once you begin doing this it's amazing how many stories you have deposited in your memory bank!

Four Sources for Content Creation

There are four sources from which to find your stories:

1. Identify the Area(s) Where You have Expertise

Referring to my 'Balance Wheel,' illuminated in detail in my book 'The Art of Significance-Achieving the Level Beyond Success,' start thinking about the experiences you've had in each of the Nine Areas of Life. Ask yourself what you know about each category and the life lessons you've learned that make you a subject matter expert in one or more of them.

Physical Fitness
Continuous Education
Deeper Spirituality
Emotional Stability
Social Networking
Family Togetherness
Financial Literacy
Fun/Hobbies/Recreation
Charitable Giving

When compelled to get yourself in better physical condition, or as a leader, you are put in an awkward position to suggest to someone else they should lose weight, the best solution to inspire the quickest response is to craft a humorous scenario or tell a story!

If you or someone else is overweight and unhealthy, ask if you look at yourself in the mirror as a 'fat failure.' If so, this is negative, counter-productive, and sabotages your belief you can change. However, if you change how you see yourself from a fat failure - to someone who has been very successful at putting on weight (Ha!), you realize you gained weight one pound at a time and can lose it one pound at a time!

Story: "Are You Physically Fit?"

When my youngest daughter was 12 years old, she competed as a dancer in competitions around the country. During an event in Denver Colorado, when she was with her mother and a fellow dance studio member with his mother, I received a frantic phone call from the young man's younger 10-year-old brother.

In a terrified voice, he explained that his dad – who for the record was a big, strong, solid, 6-foot tall, 200-pound firefighter, had fallen over on the kitchen floor, and was struggling to breathe with his eyes rolling back in his head. The young boy had called 9-1-1 and had called his mom in Denver, who told him to call the neighbor and to call me so I could meet them at the hospital, which was 90 minutes from my home.

I hung up the phone and raced in my car to get there as fast as I could. When I arrived, they still had not arrived, and the hospital was only fifteen minutes from their house. What could have gone wrong?

When they finally got to the emergency room, Dad was diagnosed as having had a stroke but had been without oxygen and the proper stroke medication for so long that there was little they could do to help him. And this amazing father, husband, public servant, and friend, died.

Was it hospital malpractice? No! When the ambulance was dispatched by the 911 operator, the two EMTs were big, overweight, out of shape, weak, and heavy-breathing men who didn't have the physical strength to lift Dad off the kitchen floor and put him on the gurney to roll him into the ambulance and transport him to the hospital. So, he lay on the kitchen floor for an hour until they could dispatch a second ambulance with a different qualified, and physically fit crew!

At the funeral there were tears of sadness mixed with feelings of anger, all because two EMTs didn't take their physical fitness seriously!

Story: "Belief Changes Reality"

Telling a story is the safest, surest way to expand beliefs, elevate expectations, and empower behavior to create lasting change.

In a study at Harvard University in the 1950s, research scientists placed rats in a pool of water to test how long they could tread water. On average, they'd give up and sink after 15 minutes. But just as their heads went under water due to exhaustion and they had given up to die, the researchers would pluck them out, dry them off, let them rest for a few minutes, and put them back in the water for a second round.

Question: in this second bout, how long do you think they lasted? Moments ago, they had swam to the point of exhaustion and sure death.

Another 5, 10 or 15 minutes? No! 60 hours of swimming! Because the rats 'believed' they would eventually be rescued; they could push their bodies way past what they previously thought impossible.

Story: "Breaking the 4-Minute Mile"

For decades, the world's top runners were convinced no one would ever run a 4-minute mile. It was physiologically impossible for a human to run that fast! But in 1954, 25-year-old Roger Bannister set a new world record of 3:59.4. Once other runners knew it could be done, 46 days later, Bannister's record was broken. A year later, three more broke it. To date, over 1,000 runners have conquered this barrier, referred to in sports, business, and life as the Bannister Effect!

In 1953, Sir Edmund Hillary's summit of Mount Everest inspired others to believe it was possible, and hundreds have scaled it since! Believing it is never too late, Ray Kroc joined McDonald's at 52. Henry Ford started Ford at 40. Harland Sanders started KFC at 65. I won my first argument against my wife at 69! Ha! It's no surprise that Henry Ford said, "If you think you can or can't, you are right!"

Story: "Leaving Your Mark"

Naomi Rhode and her husband Jim had been conducting a seminar in Hawaii. One evening, they were walking along the beach when she paused to look back to see how far they had gone. Seeing their footprints in the sand, she filled with pride commenting to her husband, "Wow, think about the countless footprints we have left in the lives of others."

Suddenly the ocean swept into shore, and the white water washed away their footprints, leaving no sign they had ever been there. Shaken, Naomi asked her husband how they could leave a more lasting impact and make a bigger difference in the lives of those whom they serve.

Jim wisely replied, "Just Walk on Higher Ground."

Chapter Eleven

Transitional Experiences and Significant Emotional Events

(Continuation of the Four Sources for Content Creation)

2. Identify the 'Transitional Experiences'

Every time you moved from school to school, graduating from high school, moving away from family or friends, starting and adjusting to college, graduating college, getting your first job, changing jobs, career moves, starting or ending a relationship, getting married, buying or selling a home, having or adopting a child, parenting an infant, child, or adolescent, empty nesting, divorce, experiencing financial gain or loss, retirement, death of a loved one.

Guaranteed, every one of them taught you something about adapting to change, facing fear, leaping into the abyss of the unknown, evaluating risk versus reward, finding the opportunity in change, why we think holding on makes us stronger when sometimes it's letting go, the reality that no matter what your past has been you have a spotless future, and 'pain is a signal to grow not to suffer. Once you learn the lesson the pain is teaching you, the pain goes away – in life, there are no mistakes, only lessons!'

Story: "A Freshman's First Letter Home"

Dear Mom,

I'm sorry it's taken me so long to write. I've never been to the city before. It's my first time away from you, and I'm trying to figure everything out. I don't live where I did when you dropped me off. I read in the paper where most accidents happen within twenty miles of where you live, so I moved.

This place had what I thought was a washing machine. The first day I put four shirts in it, I pulled the chain and haven't seen them since. I finally found the real machine and bought laundry detergent. It said, "ALL," so I dumped the whole box in. I now owe three thousand dollars for water flood damage, but they deducted three hundred dollars because the carpets on all three floors of the dorms are clean!

It only rained twice this week - three days the first time and four days the second time. The president of my fraternity fell in a whiskey vat at our last party. Some students tried to pull him out, but he fought them off gallantly and drowned. We cremated him but couldn't get the flame to go out. He burned for five days.

Three of my other friends went off a bridge in a pickup. One was driving. The other two were in the back. The driver got out. He rolled down the window and swam to safety. The other two drowned because they couldn't get the tailgate down.

Sincerely, Your Loving Son

P. S. I was going to send you the expense receipts you requested, but I already had this letter sealed.

3. Dig Deep to Uncover Your S.E.E.

Psychologists call these 'Significant Emotional Events' defined as an experience from which a person undergoes noticeable change – an isolated experience that you can quantify and measure in terms of what you thought and believed and how you acted and behaved *Before* it occurred – and how you now think and believe differently and act and behave differently *Because* it occurred. The two operative words are Before and Because.

You know when you've experienced an event like this because it shakes you to the core. It disrupts your emotional, mental, and physical well-being. An experience that is so mentally arresting that it becomes a catalyst for you to consider, examine, and possibly change your current approach to time and urgency.

To me, a Significant Emotional Event is much different and life-altering than the aforementioned 'Transitional Experiences.' Although they test us and change us, they are nothing more than temporary situations that force us to adapt to change. However, S.E.E. experiences change us forever – change our 'stars' – alter the definite course of our lives in a way we did not choose, that we cannot control. Therefore, Significant Emotional Events are the only experiences that can teach us the true steps of Resiliency – which are required for us to get back up and go again.

My personal S.E.E. experiences include my battle with cancer as an eight-year-old boy, being paralyzed in a practice tackling drill that cut short my football career, the death of my hero dad, my heart attack, my hospital battle with Covid 19, and my throat surgery that determined if I could continue as a professional speaker. What are yours? I know you have one or some.

Make a list. Identify the exact life lessons you learned from them: leave no regrets, make every day count, the goal is not to live forever – the goal is to create something that will – leave every place in better shape than you found it – leave every person saying, 'I like me best when I'm with you, I want to see you again!'

The sites, situations, people, places, and things that shape our values, move us emotionally, and change our perception into a new reality - knowing it is our values that guide our way forward through the many choices we are offered every day. When we change and up-level our values, we automatically change who we are, which changes how others view us, which changes our life!

To illustrate, let me share an experience that on the surface had nothing to do with me, but literally changed my perspective, which up-leveled my mindset and deepened my heart-set forever:

Story: "Random Acts of Kindness"

On a freezing winter's day in my hometown of Salt Lake City, Utah, I was caught in a blizzard snowstorm with the howling wind blowing the ice particles into my skin like a knife. There was only one entrance open into the shopping mall and I was standing ninth in line to enter through the turn-style revolving door.

A Salvation Army bellringer was standing bundled up in a hat, warm coat, and gloves next to his bucket, hoping each of us well-dressed businessmen would contribute to his worthy cause.

None of us moved until our selfishness was interrupted by a homeless man with no coat and bare toes protruding out the front of his worn sneakers, who stopped, reached into the pocket of his tattered pants, turned it inside out, and pulled out all of the money he had. Tears filled my frozen eyes as I watched him count out 93 cents, drop it into the red bucket, smile, and say, "Merry Christmas lad," and disappear into the foggy storm.

Obviously, I put a twenty-dollar bill in the bucket, and ever since that day over ten years ago, I've never walked past an individual who is homeless without giving him or her at least a dollar. Why? It's not about him or her. It's about making sure that I stop judging people without getting to know them, and realizing that regardless if the person who is homeless is struggling with mental illness, or is going to use the money to buy alcohol, drugs or to buy food or take care of their children, it does not matter. I will not judge them!

What matters is that I engaged in an act of selfless service, obeyed the law of acceptance, unconditionally loved, and proved to myself that I was needed.

Why did this experience change me forever? Because it illuminated two important, powerful, profound truths that I had never fully understood or felt the need to act on:

- We should always use 'Person First Language' when describing another human being. The same God who made me made him/ her too! We must never say 'the homeless beggar' but instead, refer to him as one who happens to be down on his luck and is homeless.

- In the KJV Bible, Matthew 25:35-40 eloquently reminds all of us: 'For I was thirsty, and ye gave me drink: I was a stranger, and ye took me in: Naked, and ye clothed me: I was sick, and ye visited me: Since ye have done it unto one of the least of these, my brethren, ye have done it unto me.'

Story: "Get Yourself Right"

A father came home from work and his little boy excitedly yelled, 'Let's go play ball!' But Dad had work to complete and replied, 'I don't have time right now, but I want you to know that I love you.' His son countered, "I don't want you to love me, I want you to play ball with me!'

Feeling guilty, Dad scrambled to find something to keep his son occupied for an hour so he could finish his work.

On the coffee table lay a magazine with a cover picture of a map of the world. Dad quickly ripped the map into numerous tiny pieces, gave the pieces to his young son, and instructed him that as soon as he had put the map back together, they would go outside and play.

His boy left the room and Dad got to work. But to his surprise, fifteen minutes later, the son was back, and the puzzle was assembled. Amazed, the father asked how he finished so quickly.

"It was easy," his boy explained. On the other side of the map was a picture of a man. Once I got the man right, the whole world was right!"

Chapter Twelve

Converting Your Bucket List into a 'Living List'

(Continuation of the Four Sources for Content Creation)

'Our deepest fear is not that we are inadequate.
Our deepest fear is that we are powerful beyond measure.
It is our light, not our darkness that most frightens us.
Your playing small does not serve the world.
There is nothing enlightened about shrinking
so that other people won't feel insecure around you.
As we are liberated from our own fear,
our presence automatically liberates others.'
- Marianne Williamson

4. Create Your Own Extraordinary Experiences

To make you more credible to learn from, more fascinating to listen to, and more inspiring to be around.

There are three simple steps to create your own experiences. First, look around, be present, and stay aware of the random teaching moments and experiences that are continuously revealing themselves to you during the day. Evaluate their life-changing messages and write them down as a story so you can share them in a speech one day.

Story: "Dead Deer"

For example, during one particularly long, harsh winter, the snowfall in Utah was so deep that it forced the deer population out of the mountains and down into the city parks and residential areas in search of food. Because the deer were stranded, state wildlife agencies immediately brought in truckloads of hay and spread it in the fields around our neighborhood so the deer could eat. One week later more than a hundred dead deer were lying in the streets. Why?

When the veterinarians performed autopsies, they discovered that the stomachs of the deer were full of hay. The deer had eaten plenty of food, but they had not been nourished. They got what they thought they wanted at the moment, but they died because they didn't get what they truly needed.

Story: "Thermostat"

Second, notice objects, instruments, and operating systems that could be crafted into analogies and metaphorical teaching tools. For example, a thermostat is a component of an HVAC (heating and air conditioning) control system that senses the difference between actual temperature and desired *set-point* temperature. It's an instrument that focuses on inside conditions, measuring changes in circumstances that allow us to accurately predict and expect what the temperature will be. The moment you set the thermostat, it triggers a furnace or air conditioner to run at full capacity until the set-point temperature is reached. Then it shuts off the equipment until it's needed again.

In terms of our human set point, it is always dialed into the level of our self-esteem, sense of self-worth, and degree of personal development.

For example, how many times have we seen someone win 100 million dollars in the lottery only to be completely broke three years later? How many people do we know who go on a crazy diet and lose fifty pounds or more, but six months later they have gained all the weight back and more? More devastating, how many times do we see a wonderful woman doing everything she knows how to do to get out of a physically and emotionally abusive relationship, only to jump back into a more dysfunctional relationship with a bigger loser than the bum she just kicked out? Why is this?

It is simply because of their personal thermostat. No matter what happens on the outside with money, weight, relationships, promotions of authority, and so forth, ultimately our thermostat is going to kick in to bring our outside world to match our internal set point. In order to accumulate more in the outside world, the key to this equation is to *become* more on the inside.

Story: "What Goes Around Comes Around"

Third, make a Bucket List that rekindles your passion, triggers your creativity, and unlocks your imagination to include amazing things you would like to accomplish, remarkable people you want to meet and interview, and incredible adventures you want to experience. Then, make a list of individuals who have connections to each item on your list, and who can introduce you to the right person who has the right connections to help you turn this Bucket List into a reality. Then, research these individuals to discover what their 'hot button' is and how you can serve them.

My mentor Zig Ziglar taught, 'We can get anything in life that we want when we are willing to help enough other people get what they want.' This belief fueled the creation of my dynamic and ever-expanding Bucket List that I knew could become a 'Living List' through a commitment to Service Before Self.

Therefore, since July of 2001, I have given over 350 free speeches to the United States Military, including hundreds at Air University, keynotes at the Four Star 'Corona' Conferences, at every MAJCOM Commander's Conference, and have conducted eight Military Tours 'down range' to our combat troops in different AOR's around the world.

Consequently, I was asked to serve as a Pentagon Appointee on the National Civic Leaders Board with the Secretary of the Air Force.

Eventually, with the Generals knowing my speaker's honorarium, and that I'd never asked the military for compensation, the Generals offered me opportunities to fly the aircraft they had in their command.

Add to this the list of goals I created to learn from experts who could turn decades into days, work with superstars who would build my celebrity, and what I already knew from being a Golden Gloves boxing champion, an alpine ski racing, and motocross champion, racing automobiles at Nürburgring, and carrying the Olympic Torch in the Winter Games - and I have positioned myself as one who does more than teach what I know. I teach who I am, how I live, what I've done – showing that through service before self, you can live a 'Bucket List' life!

- Flying the T-38, F-4, F-15, F-16, F-18 fighter jets at Mach 2
- Flying with the Air Force Thunderbirds performing all acrobatic maneuvers in the air show, catching 9.4 Gs at Mach 1
- Flying an F-16, in air-to-air 'dogfighting' with another F-16
- Flying the B-52, B-2 (Spirit #532), and B-1 bomber
- Flying the U2, KC-10, C-5, C-17, C-130 & KC-135 Refueler
- Flying Blackhawk Helicopters over Baghdad at 100 feet
- Taking off and Landing on the USS Harry S. Truman Aircraft Carrier and piloting it from the Admirals 'Bridge' for 30 mins
- Speaking to Nato Commanders in the Grand Ballroom of Saddam Hussein's Baghdad Palace, staying in his Guest House
- Being shot at in a Chinook in Afghanistan (caught on GoPro!)
- Attending three sacred "Dignified Transfers' at Dover AFB and ministering to the heartbroken families at Fisher House.

Chapter Thirteen

The Rules of Story Creation, Editing and Telling

'We are, as a species, addicted to stories. Even when the body goes to sleep, the mind stays up all night, telling itself stories. Stories were crucial to our evolution - more so than opposable thumbs that let us hang on; stories told us what to hang on to." – Lisa Cron

The '4 Cs' and '4 Ps' of Storytelling

Just as a skilled architect follows a blueprint to construct a magnificent building, storytellers employ the '4 Cs' and '4 Ps' as a framework to craft compelling narratives. These fundamental elements are essential pillars that ensure the success of any story, be it a novel, film, or marketing campaign.

The process of writing a powerful, memorable story begins by creating a 'Storyboard.' We trigger our passion, creativity, and imagination by segregating the Storyboard into two Sections of Four of 4Cs and 4 Ps:

4Cs:

Concept
What is the 'distilled' message – the one big idea worth sharing?

Characters

Every story needs a protagonist hero that everybody can cheer on, who introduces and champions your Concept. And an antagonist who is the nemesis that creates and perpetuates the disagreeing conflict and obstacles the protagonist must overcome. *(More explanation to follow).*

Conflict

What is the one problem you are going to solve? Why does the controversy exist? What are the serious consequences if you don't solve it?

Context

What is the setting? Situational awareness of time, people, place, and things? Describe the environment: indoors, outdoors, city, country, social, economic, business, political, sports competition, family experience.

4Ps:

Plot

The plot forms the backbone of a gripping story. It comprises the sequence of events, conflicts, and resolutions that push the narrative forward, keeping the audience emotionally engaged to discover what happens next.

People

Memorable complex, relatable, and multi-dimensional characters are the backbone of every story, creating empathetic connections with the readers and listeners.

Pacing

The best writers know how to balance exposition, dialogue, contemplative moments, and action to create an emotional and intellectual roller coaster ride that maintains the audience's interest and emotional involvement throughout the journey.

Purpose

Whether the goal is to entertain, inspire, educate, or persuade, a well-defined purpose drives the narrative forward and gives meaning to the story's characters, conflicts, and resolutions

Nine Ingredients for Writing Iconic Stories

As I researched the art and science of storytelling, every professor of creative writing and professional storyteller referred to the amazing Disney Pixar Studios, which is arguably one of the greatest storytelling enterprises of our generation. Thus, I have amalgamated my ideas and experience (having been published in more than 50 million books, in 50 languages worldwide) with the most significant truths on Pixar's long list of time-tested suggestions. My goal is to help you bring your stories to life, blending the joy of imagination and creativity with the exhilaration of sharing!

1. Find your Story. Every story starts with a spark of curiosity. Stories can come from memories, dreams, or even a question like, 'What if?' Think of moments that moved you, characters that made you laugh, or places you've seen that you can still picture in your mind. A story doesn't have to be epic, because even simple tales can become meaningful when they come from a place of wonder!

2. Set the Scene. Stories come alive when the setting feels as real as the characters. Describe the place where your story unfolds that triggers the senses. Is it a winding cliffside, a quiet forest, or a cozy room with a fire blazing to warm you as you feed your soul with a romance novel on a cold winter night? Evoking sights, sounds, and even smells can draw readers/listeners into the world of your story. Using vivid, sensory language paints a word picture as in: 'The crisp air smelled of pine and cinnamon.'

3. Create a Clear Structure and Purpose. Pixar uses the story structure created by professional playwright and improviser Kenn Adams. To write and tell a compelling, entertaining story, Pixar recommends Adam's 'Story Spine.'

   Ask and answer the following questions in this order. Fill in the blanks to put your thoughts and feelings into a specific sequential order.

   THE STORY SPINE:

   Once upon a time there was [fill in the blank________].

   Every day, ________.

   One day, ________.

   Because of that, ________.

   Until finally, ________.

4. Trigger your Passion, Creativity, and Imagination using All Five Key Ingredients in every story:

Message. Why must you tell THIS story? What's the belief burning within you that your story feeds off? What greater purpose does this serve? What does it teach? What is the 'punchline' and 'moral' to the story? Be specific on how and when we will know the Hero wins.

Hero. The Protagonist presents and defends the message. The champion of your cause, knowing we love a good underdog to root for, and the audience admires a character for trying more than for their success, battling against all odds, on the 'Hero's journey.

Villain. The Antagonist person, adversarial idea, or negative circumstance that creates pain and obstacles to overcome. The reason the Hero needs to step up and fight.

Dialogue. Create a conversation between the Hero and the Villain, about the negative situation and the possible solution. Give them distinct personalities and opinions, with a unique voice or accent when speaking, and a favorite phrase they say. Add humor, argument, philosophical debate, psychological manipulation, metaphor, simile, statistics, quotes, etc.

Conclusion / Resolution. Come up with your ending before you figure out your middle. Conclusions are hard, so get yours working up front by beginning with the end in mind, proving that good always prevails over evil. Through perseverance, the Hero wins! Then, reverse engineer to write a story that ends in this message.

5. Appeal to our Deepest Emotions. Psychologists generally agree that there are six basic emotions: anger, disgust, fear, happiness, sadness, and surprise. Watch the Pixar move 'Inside Out,' and you'll recognize these emotions as the six characters in the movie.

6. Bring your Characters to life. Characters are the heart of every story and bringing them to life is key to capturing your audience. Think of them as old friends with a back story for why they think and behave the way they do. Add small vivid details, knowing characters are more memorable when they are imperfect, like we are!

7. Be Fresh and Unpredictable. We are tired of the damsel in distress with Prince Charming saving her. What makes a story compelling is when our perception of reality is challenged in a clever way.

8. Power Through 'Writer's Block. If you're stuck on coming up with something truly unique, get rid of the 1st thing that comes to mind – and then the 2nd, 3rd, 4th, and 5th. Challenge yourself to dig deep.

9. Create a Rhythm and Pace that keeps readers/listeners engaged and intrigued. Vary your sentences with shorter ones that create excitement with your tone and volume, using 'punctuating pauses' and inflection to create moments of calm, tension, and anticipation!

To illustrate how these Nine Ingredients interface with one another, let me share one of my iconic stories:

Story: "Art Collection"

A father and son were very close and enjoyed adding valuable art pieces to their collection. Priceless works by Picasso, Van Gogh, Monet, and many other artists adorned the walls of the family estate. The son's trained eye and sharp business mind caused his widowed father to beam with pride as they dealt with art collectors around the world.

As winter approached, war engulfed the nation, and the young man left to serve his country. After only a few short weeks, his father received a telegram. His beloved son had died while rushing a fellow soldier to a medic. Distraught and lonely, the old man faced the future with anguish and sadness.

One morning, a knock on the door awakened the depressed old man. As he opened the door, he was greeted by a soldier with a large package in his hand who said, "I was a friend of your son. I was the one he was rescuing when he died. May I come in for a few moments? I have something to show you." As the two began to talk, the soldier explained that his son spoke highly of the love he and his dad shared for fine art. "I'm an artist," said the soldier, "So I want to give you this."

As the old man unwrapped the package, he found a portrait of his son. Overcome with emotion, the man thanked the soldier, promising to hang the picture above the fireplace.

As soon as the soldier had departed, the old man removed the Rembrandt from the wall and replaced it with his new more meaningful masterpiece, telling his neighbors it was his most prized possession.

The following spring, the old man passed away. The art world waited in anticipation for his paintings to be sold at an auction. The day soon arrived, and collectors from around the world gathered to bid on some of the world's most spectacular paintings.

The auction began with a painting that was not on the printed list - the portrait of the man's son. The auctioneer asked for an opening bid.

The room was silent. "Who will open the bidding with one hundred dollars?" he asked. Minutes passed. No one spoke. Finally, a man yelled, "Who cares about that painting? Let's get on to the good stuff."

More voices echoed in agreement. "No, we have to sell this one first," replied the auctioneer. "Now, who will take the son?" Finally, a friend of the old man spoke. "Will you take ten dollars for the painting? I knew the boy, so I'd like to have it."

The auctioneer called, "Going once, going twice. Sold."

The gavel fell. Cheers filled the room and someone exclaimed, "Now we can start bidding on these treasures!"

But the auctioneer announced the auction was over. Stunned disbelief quieted the room. A woman pleaded, "What do you mean it's over? There are millions of dollars of art here!"

The auctioneer replied, "It's very simple. According to the will of the Father, whoever takes the Son gets it all."

Power in the Punchline. Story: "My Top Gun"

My first opportunity to fly a fighter jet occurred at PAX River Naval Station. On arrival, I received a physical and asked the Wing Commander what I should eat before my flight. He recommended bananas. Why? He said they taste the same coming up as they do going down!

After a morning of training, we were airborne for 90 minutes, doing aileron rolls, loops, and dive-bombing, catching 7 Gs, at Mach II.

When we landed, a journalist asked if I popped my cookies. Let me say the Commander was right about the bananas, and I ejected a box of Milk Duds I had eaten at a movie when I was nine! I was upside down so long that I think I'm the only person who has ever thrown down! When I asked the Commander how we flew this magnificent high-tech machine, he said, "By feel - you become the plane. *When you climbed up the ladder, did you strap into the F-18, or strap the F-18 onto you?*"

Chapter Fourteen

The Art of Embellishing with Quotes, Humor and Emotion

(Make Them Think, Laugh, Cry)

"To me, there are three things we all should do every day of our lives. Number one is Laugh. You should laugh every day. Number two is Think. You should spend some time in thought. And number three is, you should have your Emotions moved to tears, could be happiness or joy. But think about it. If you laugh, you think, and you cry, that's a full day. That's a heck of a day. You do those seven days a week, you're going to have something special." – Jimmy Valvano

In 1983, Jimmy Valvano, head basketball coach at North Carolina State University that won the National NCAA Basketball Championship in 1983. He continued to coach and eventually became one of the most beloved ESPN Sports Analysts on TV. In 1993, Valvano was in a very public battle against cancer and was presented the Arthur Ashe Courage Award at the ESPYs, which led to him delivering an unforgettable acceptance speech known as 'Don't Give Up, Don't Ever Give Up!'

Sadly, Coach Valvano passed away from cancer a few weeks later. Among the priceless nuggets of wisdom, he shared in what would be the last speech he ever delivered, the one thing he mentioned that resonated with me as a professional speaker and storyteller has become my formula for crafting a speech listener's love and creating a story everybody loves listening to.

Since then, I have dedicated my life to this formula, and it works! Every day for me, is a heck of a day! And because it has had such an amazing impact on my daily attitude and personal performance as a professor, author, and speaker, I have taken it one step further. From an audience member's perspective, I want every speaker I listen to, to make every speech funny, provocative (by adding quotes), and emotional. When they do, that's a heck of a speech! When we can implement this formula in a story, that's a heck of a story!

To show you exactly how this works, let me share one of my famous iconic stories:

I attended the University of Utah with an 87-year-old woman named Rose. I met her one day in my chemistry class. We became friends. During the school year Rose became a legend on campus, organizing student gatherings in the middle of campus to chit-chat while eating lunch. I invited her to speak at our football banquet at the end of the year. She graduated. But suddenly died a couple of weeks after the Commencement Ceremony.

That's it! That's the story! Is it compelling? Did I keep you interested? Did I teach you anything? Did I demonstrate the reason why I needed to share it with you? Most significantly, was it funny, provocative, or emotional? Absolutely not!

So… the following is my well-thought-out, edited, embellished version that will make you laugh, think, and feel. I have highlighted the humor in Bold and Underlined the evocative quotes and the emotional messaging. When you finish reading this story, pause to evaluate what I have done and apply it to one of the current stories I have already told. Then, to help you master this technique, use it to help you improve a new story you are currently working on!

Story: "Rose"

On the first day of school, our professor introduced himself to our chemistry class and challenged us to get to know someone we did not know. I stood up to look around when a gentle hand touched my shoulder. I turned around to find a wrinkled older lady with a giant smile that lit up her entire face like a Christmas tree. She said, **"Hi, handsome, my name is Rose. I am eighty-seven years old. Do you want to get lucky?"**

I laughed and enthusiastically replied, "You gorgeous babe, of course I do! Why are you in college at your young, innocent age?"

She kidded, "I'm here looking for a rich husband, you know, get married, have a couple of children, then retire and travel."

Hysterically laughing, I begged her to be serious. Her answer was simple but profound. <u>"I always dreamed of having a college degree and so I'm getting one!"</u>

After class, we walked to the student union building and shared a chocolate milkshake. It was obvious we were soul mates, and we became instant friends. In fact, every day for the next three months, we left class together, walked to the union building, and for at least an hour, I sat there in total awe listening to this "time machine" share her life experiences with me.

<u>Clearly, wisdom is the gift of the elderly. When an old woman dies an entire library burns to the ground!</u>

Over the course of the school year, Rose became a campus icon and generated attention everywhere she went. **She loved to dress up and even occasionally wore miniskirts and high heels! In the third week of school, she even got a tiny tattoo above her left breast. I teased her that I was hurt it didn't say "Dan My Man."** <u>Of course, it was a magnificent rose.</u>

Every day around 12 o'clock noon, Rose would pause in the library plaza to take a break from walking and attending classes. Within moments a crowd of 50 to 100 students would gather around her to hear and feel the wisdom of Rose. I will never forget the day <u>she taught us that we don't see things as they are – we see things as we are, when she lovingly and tactfully interacted with one of our coed friends who had lost her hair in her battle with leukemia.</u>

Rose complimented Melody in front of all of us by acknowledging that she never complains and then asked her if there was a difference between dying of cancer and living with cancer, and what was it going to be for her? Whoa! I don't think anyone ever complained about having a 'bad hair day' or took life for granted again!

Rose was so inspirational that I invited her to speak at our football banquet, and I'll never forget what she said. When I introduced her and she stepped to the podium, she inadvertently dropped her speech and her 3x5 cards hit the floor. Frustrated and a bit embarrassed, she leaned into the microphone and simply said, **"I'm sorry I'm so nervous. I gave up beer for Lent and this whiskey is killing me!** I'll never get my speech back together, so let me just tell you what I know."

As we laughed, she cleared her throat and began, "There are only four secrets to staying young, being authentically happy, and achieving lasting success. It doesn't matter if you're a football player, a professor, a business professional, or an old lady like me. We all need to:

"(1) Carpe diem with humor. Seize each day with laughter. **For example, my best friend started walking five miles a day when she was sixty years old. She's ninety-seven now, and we don't know where she is! Ha! On a personal note, my late husband and I enjoyed seventeen great years of marriage. Seventeen out of fifty-five ain't bad! Every night I said the same prayer: 'Dear Lord, I pray for wisdom to understand my man, love to forgive him, and patience to handle his moods. Because Lord, if I pray for strength, I will beat the hell out of him!' Haha!"**

"(2) As I've walked around this college campus this year I noticed how many of you football players were still wearing your old high school athletic letter jackets. **I wanted to stop every one of you and say, "I know you used to be a stud muffin hunk of burnin' love, but when your horse dies, dismount! Stop living in your past. Get a new horsey. Getty up young man.** Remember the ten two letter words: If it is to be it is up to me. And remember that the only person you need to be better than is the person you were yesterday!"

"(3) <u>Treat everybody you meet with dignity and respect and make them better because they met you. The same God who made you, made me too!</u>"

"(4) <u>Leave no regrets. There is a giant difference between growing older and growing up. If you are nineteen years old and lie in bed for one full year, and don't do one productive thing, you will turn twenty years old. If I am eighty-seven years old and stay in bed for a year, I will turn eighty-eight. Whoop-de-do! Anybody can grow older.</u>

<u>That doesn't take any talent or ability. The idea is to grow up. The elderly usually don't have regrets for what we did, but rather for things we did not do. The only people who fear death are those with regrets.</u>"

At year's end, Rose's life-long dream of graduating from college had become a reality. <u>As she walked across the stage to receive her diploma the arena erupted into an epic standing ovation. Unbeknownst to anyone, Rose had been battling cancer for some time, and one week after graduation, Rose died peacefully in her sleep.</u>

<u>More than two thousand college students attended her funeral in tribute to this Wonder Woman who never did anything famous and never made a lot of money. Through her example, she simply taught us that it's never too late to be all you can possibly be!</u>

Think

When it comes to getting people to 'think' we need to either challenge the status quo, not by merely asking a question, but by questioning the answer - or embellish and deepen one's current understanding with a quotable quip.

For example, when my Keynote is on the Art of Significance-Achieving the Level Beyond Success, I need to challenge what my listeners believe, or I can't take them to the next level and fulfill my promise. Consequently, I always quote Alvin Toffler:

"The illiterate of the 21st century will not be those who cannot read and write, but those who cannot learn, unlearn, and relearn."

Then, I follow it up with a deeper explanation of the eternal change in beliefs I experienced during my adventure to the edge of space in the U2:

"I could see the thin delicate Ozone where the blue turns to the blackness of space and realized it's not my air, my water, and my world. But in fact, it is Our air, Our water, and Our collective Stewardship to take better care of Our Mother Earth – as literal brothers and sisters in the family of humanity – working together in our global economy.

Needless to say – this high flight changed my life forever. How? Why? It forever changed my Perspective - which controls everything we believe and do. Let me give you some quick examples:

Is your glass half empty or half full - or is it Refillable? It's perspective.

If we are all looking at the same rainstorm and someone Complains "What a horrible day' – and someone else Exclaims 'What a wonderful day' – the weather did not change! We don't see things as They are – we see things as We are! It's perspective.

And my last example. Let's say this side of my hand is painted white, and this side is painted blue. What color is my hand? Who is right? You all are – depending on your perspective.

For us to communicate at our deepest, most authentic levels of empathy and total understanding, we need to be willing to come around to the other side of the hand to see the other person's perspective and acknowledge that, yes, it is white or blue. Which turns an opinion of who is right into agreeing on what is right. When we expand our beliefs and level up our perspective, we change our reality and inspire others to also Think bigger than ever before!

When I share my 'Signature Story' about recovering from my paralyzing injury that cut short my football career, I explain that I didn't start to recover until I stopped competing against others, focusing on fame and fortune, and started competing only against what I was capable of, focusing on purpose and being whole. This is the perfect time to interrupt my 'flow' and insert two quotes that make my listeners think more deeply about my messages of Self-Competition and Purpose:

"Everyone is a genius. But if you judge a fish by its ability to climb a tree, it will live its whole life believing that it is stupid." – Albert Einstein

"The two most important days in your life are the day you are born, and the day you find out why." – Mark Twain

Laugh

(When you want to immediately connect, use self-deprecating humor):
'I'm so old I bend over to pull up my socks and think, 'What else can I accomplish while I'm way down here?'

'I struggled in school with dyslexia, which kept me from religion because I had a hard time worshipping Dog!'

(If you're talking about the necessity to think on your feet):
'A Manager was called into the CEO's office and told, 'We are giving you a raise and a promotion and moving you to Detroit to run the operation.' The guy complains, 'I don't want to go to Detroit! The only thing there are ugly women and bad hockey teams!' The CEO says, 'Really? My wife is from Detroit.' The guy responds, 'Which team does she play for?'

(If you want to laugh about the consequences of settling for cheap):
'My schedule required that I book myself on Spirit Airlines. Yikes! When we hit cruising altitude, the flight attendant announced there was a medical emergency on the plane and asked if there was a doctor on board who could help. I couldn't help but laugh! There are no doctors on a Spirit Airlines plane. They all fly Delta!

A moment later, the flight attendant made another announcement, asking if there was any medical personnel on the plane. I laughed again.

There are no medical personnel flying on Spirit Airlines. The tickets cost 39 dollars! Every passenger is unemployed! Ha!

In desperation, the flight attendant lowered the standard and begged, 'Has anyone recently watched 'Grey's Anatomy' on TV? To which a young girl yelled, 'No, but I was a nurse for Halloween!' The flight attendant replied, 'Then get up here and help us out!' Ha!

(When speaking at a conference, and they hold a golf tournament for attendees):
How many of you golfed today? I love golf, but I'm not good. I lose balls in the ball washer! You think you had a tough year? I had to get my ball retriever regripped! The good news is that I'm writing two new books, 'How To Line Up Your Fifth Putt.' And 'Awesome Second Shots Off The Lady's Tee.'

It was no surprise that your sales champion _____ won the tournament today. He plays so much golf he actually gathers friends together to show them slides of work! Today, I played with your CEO _____, and on #9 he hit a massive tee shot! 'Hey, I don't drive that far on vacation!' Then, on the green, I left my three-foot putt short, and your Senior VP _____ whispered, 'Nice lag, at least you had the right club!' So, what did I learn today? 'If you're having a hard time meeting new people, just try picking up the wrong golf ball!' Ha!

Cry

To illustrate how we bring emotion into our speeches and stories, let me take you back to why and how Coach Jimmy Valvano's ESPY speech had such a powerful, long-lasting impact on everyone who heard it.

Story: "Unstoppable"

In 2012 a young man named Anthony Robles, born with only one leg, won the National NCAA Wrestling Championship and was honored as the recipient of the 2012 Jimmy Valvano ESPY Award for Courage.

Anthony phoned me and asked if I would write his acceptance speech. I immediately flew into Phoenix, Arizona, and interviewed him and his mother for five hours where we Googled Jimmy Valvano to get an idea of why this prestigious award was named after him.

Fast-forward to the ESPYs as Anthony walked out on stage to a standing ovation from iconic sports superstars. He humbly honored his mother for never giving up on him, even though it would be difficult to raise a son with only one leg and easier to put him up for adoption.

At the beginning of his wrestling career, he lost most of his matches, and people said, 'It's okay. You tried.' This ticked him off so badly! Losing is not okay! What they were really saying was that he was a handicapped kid and should be grateful that he could even participate.

Anthony has now dedicated his life to inspiring others as a Motivational Speaker and Coach, closing his ESPY acceptance speech with a short poem I wrote that captures the essence of Anthony, which is now the Title of an incredible Netflix film on his inspirational story:

"UNSTOPPABLE"

Every soul who comes to earth
With a leg or two at birth
Must wrestle his opponents knowing
It's not what is, it's what can be
that measures worth.
Make it hard, just make it possible
And through pain, I'll not complain
My spirit is unconquerable.
Fearless I will face each foe
For I know I am capable.
Making winning personal
I don't care what's probable
Through blood, sweat, and tears,
I am Unstoppable!
(Copyright Dan Clark 2012)

Chapter Fifteen

Vocabulary, Descriptors, and Punchlines

"Words have energy and power to hurt, to hinder, to humiliate, to hypnotize, to help, to heal, to hug, to highlight, and to hoist." -Y. Berg

The first step in creative writing is to continuously improve our Vocabulary. Why? As you broaden your access to beautiful words, you become better able to describe your vision, ideas, specific settings, and emotional feelings. A strong vocabulary enhances communication skills and helps you develop critical thinking abilities because words are the building blocks of thought. Being able to 'say what you mean' is dependent on a robust repertoire of nouns, active verbs, and adjectives that allow you to clearly express yourself with greater passion and precision and appear more confident and persuasive.

Class Alert! There are three negative, unacceptable traits that people with a weak vocabulary share: the overuse of the words 'Like' and 'Literally,' Freezing Up in Conversations, and Stooping to the Vulgarity Level of Dropping the 'F-Bomb!' An occasional and carefully placed 'shit, damn, or hell' to accentuate a point or trigger a laugh is acceptable. But there is Never an appropriate place or reason to take the Lord's name in vain or use the 'F-word' in a speech or in a conversation! This is the #1 sign of a pathetically shallow vocabulary and diminishes the credibility and sophistication of the fool who thinks it makes them hip!

Once you engage in continuously increasing your vocabulary, you are ready to write unforgettable stories that teach timeless truths through fiction and non-fiction using my five-step process:

Five-Step Creative Process

1. **Begin with the End in Mind.** Before you begin a story-writing session, find a quiet, inspiring place that stimulates passion, creativity, and imagination until you create the punch line, or as we call it, the Point of View. It's the big idea, the lead of your story, and most importantly, the phrase that signifies the biggest change in how you want your listener to think or act about your topic. It's knowing your punch line, your ending, and that everything you're saying from the first sentence to the last is leading to a singular goal.

2. **Make Me Care.** Logic makes you think, emotion makes you act. Get readers/listeners to care so much about your message that they'll take that action out of fear and uncertainty coupled with the urgency to drive change.   It's important for logic to be present as well, but emotion is the primary motivator.

3. **Make Me Work.** As humans, we are natural problem-solvers who desperately try to bridge the gap between what we know and what we don't. So, instead of laying all your information out there, good storytelling is the well-organized absence of information – that draws us in and makes us want to know more to deduce and figure things out.

4. **Edit So Every Word Pays Its Own Way.** Once you've written the story, it's time to 'romance the language' by replacing the common, mundane verbs with gripping, action verbs that paint a textured "word picture" that makes your character or the scene come alive:

   - If you "led" a company project, replace it with Chaired, Orchestrated.

- If you "developed" and "introduced" a project into your company, use: Engineered, Launched, Pioneered, Spearheaded.

- If you helped your team operate more efficiently and "saved" money, replace it with: Deducted, Diagnosed, Reconciled.

- If your work "increased" the company's profitability, use Accelerated, Amplified, Boosted, Outpaced, Stimulated.

- If you led the company's "conversion" from an analog system to digital use: Overhauled, Remodeled, Revitalized, Streamlined.

- Instead of "leading a team" or "managing employees," use terms like Coached, Aligned, Fostered, Mobilized, Shaped, Unified.

- Because you were "responsible for," use: Forged, Navigated, Partnered, Secured.

- Because "customer service" is not a department, but a way of life, your job should be described as one who: Advocates, Arbitrates, Dispatches, Monitors, Screens, Scrutinizes.

- When your job is to "research" and "analyze," use: Audit, Calculate, Explore, Forecast, Quantify, Track.

- When asked to "describe" and "explain" what you learned in a training meeting, say you were: Briefed, Counseled, Critiqued, and Coaxed so you would Campaign what they Composed.

- When you "hit" your goals, "reach" your sales quota, and "win" a coveted department award, describe your accomplishments using: Outperformed, Showcased, Surpassed.

5 **Think Like a Hit Songwriter,** who can consolidate an entire experience into a 3-minute, 40-second song that includes a catchy, money-line 'hook' at the end of the chorus like: 'Drink, Swear, Steal and Lie,' 'Live Like You're Dying,' 'God Bless the USA.' It's this

'hook' that makes it a hit – it's the 'punchline' that turns a message into an unforgettable masterpiece! Evaluate five of my stories:

Story: "Broken Doll"

A young girl was leaving for school, and her mother reminded her to come straight home when her last class ended. Thirty minutes late, she finally walked through the front door. Her mother scolded her. 'Where have you been?' she asked. 'I've been worried sick.'

The daughter sweetly replied, 'I walked home with my friend, Sally, and she dropped her doll and it shattered to pieces. It was just awful!'

Her mother inquired, 'So you were late because you stayed to help her pick up the pieces of the doll and put it back together again?'

'Oh no, Mommy,' she explained. 'I didn't know how to fix the doll. *I just stayed to help her cry!'*

Story: "Always Look on the Bright Side"
(Crafted into a song by songwriter Don Schlitz, recorded by Kenny Rogers - 'The Greatest')

A father went to a park to play ball with his son. 'Show me what you can do,' the father said. The little boy shuffled his feet, threw the ball up in the air, took a swing, and missed. Dad counted, 'Strike one.'

The boy threw the ball up again, took a second swing, and missed again. Dad counted, 'Strike two.'

More determined than ever, the boy dug in, threw the ball higher, and took a third mighty swing, stumbling to the ground. Dad counted, 'Strike three, you're out. What do you think?'

The youngster stood up, brushed himself off, and proudly replied, *'Man, am I a good pitcher!'*

Story: "Puppies for Sale"
(I wrote this when I was 13 years old - made into an award-winning short film at Paramount Studios starring Jack Lemmon and Jesse James, musical score by Elmer Bernstein)

A store owner was tacking a sign above his door that read 'Puppies for Sale.' Signs like that have a way of attracting small children, and, sure enough, a little boy appeared under the store owner's sign. 'How much are you going to sell the puppies for?' he asked.

The store owner replied, 'Anywhere from thirty to fifty dollars.'

The little boy reached into his pocket and pulled out some change. 'I have two dollars and thirty-seven cents,' he said. 'Can I please look at them?'

The store owner smiled and whistled, and out of the kennel came Lady, who ran down the aisle of his store followed by five tiny balls of fur. One puppy was lagging considerably behind. Immediately, the little boy singled out the lagging, limping puppy and said, 'What's wrong with that little dog?'

The store owner explained that the veterinarian had examined the little puppy and had discovered it didn't have a hip socket. It would always limp. It would always be lame.

The little boy became excited. 'That is the little puppy that I want to buy.'

The store owner said, 'No, you don't want to buy that little dog. If you really want him, I'll just give him to you.'

The little boy got upset. He looked straight into the store owner's eyes, pointed his finger, and said, 'I don't want you to just give him to me. That little dog is worth every bit as much as all the other dogs and I'll pay full price. In fact, I'll give you two dollars and thirty-seven cents now and fifty cents a month until I have him paid for.'

The store owner countered, 'You really don't want to buy this little dog. He is never going to be able to run and jump and play with you like the other puppies.'

To this, the little boy reached down and rolled up his pant leg to reveal a badly twisted, crippled left leg supported by a big metal brace. He looked up at the store owner and softly replied, 'Well, I don't run so well myself and this little puppy *will need someone who understands.*'

Story: "It's What's on the Inside"

One day in New York's Central Park, a salesman was selling his balloons, often releasing a brightly colored balloon into the sky to attract attention.

Suddenly, a young, shy, African American girl asked him a question. "Mister, if you let a black balloon go, will it rise too?"

"Sweetheart," he explained. "It doesn't matter what color the balloon is. It's not what's on the outside that makes it go up.

It's what's on the inside that makes it rise."

Story: "The Last Game"

It was the final game of Brian's senior year, and a message came that his father had just died. When the coach found out, he pulled Brian aside to tell him before the game, knowing he wouldn't elect to play. But instead of reacting sorrowfully, Brian just took it all in stride and said, "I'll leave right after the game."

The coach had heard Brian speak highly of his father and expected him to grieve. When he didn't, the coach said, "Brian, you don't have to play. This game isn't that important."

Brian ignored him and played the game anyway. And play he did. Brian was the star, relentlessly running, never tiring, scoring touchdowns and almost single-handedly winning the game!

In the locker room, his teammates offered condolences, but most were appalled at his lack of sorrow. The coach was angry and worried that he had taught over-devotion to sports and not enough compassion. He scolded Brian, "Why did you play the game? Your father is dead. I'm ashamed of you and of myself."

Brian replied, "Coach, this was our last game. I am a senior. I had to play. This was the first time my dad had ever seen me play, and I had to play like I never played before."

The coach didn't understand. "What do you mean?"

With tears streaming down his cheeks, Brian replied,

"You didn't know my father was blind, did you?"

Chapter Sixteen

The Nine Types of Storytelling and Their Benefits

"I was standing at the counter, I was waitin' for the change
When I heard that old familiar music start
It was like a lighted match had been tossed into my soul
It was like a dam had broken in my heart
After taking every detour gettin' lost and losin' track
So that even if I wanted I could not find my way back
After drivin' out the memory of the way things might have been
After I'd forgotten all about us - The song remembers when."
– (recorded by Tricia Yearwood)

There are Nine Types of storytelling and Six Major Benefits that come from telling organizational stories:

1. Teaching Tales

Instead of telling someone that communication is a two-way conversation, seeking first to understand and then to be understood, tell them a tale: A young mother is in her living room talking on the phone when she looks out the window and sees her little four-year-old son standing on the curb with cars whipping by. Somehow, he had managed to open the front door and wander to the street. Frantically, she dropped the phone and ran outside to save him. Just as he was stepping out into oncoming traffic, she grabbed him and pulled him close to her. Angry, she held him at arm's length and scolded, 'How many times have I told you, don't go by the curb?'

Frightened with tears streaming down his cheeks her little guy whimpers, 'Mommy, what's a curb?'

2. Personal Stories

We are all forever in the process of composing our personal histories. The stories we weave about our own lives help us to remember them, to make sense of them, to find meaningful patterns in them, and sometimes to change them. Psychologists observe that human beings have a 'narrative need,' for arranging events into meaningful patterns of cause and effect. Paying attention to how we weave our own stories can really make a difference in how happily we live our lives, not to mention in how readily we achieve our goals.

3. Family Stories

Family stories often serve as the oral history of a family, preserving the collected wisdom of its experiences, and the passing along its traditions. Stories about our ancestors give us a way to define our family's identity: they tell us what it means to be a Clark or a Hatch or a McCulloch. Often, these stories embody the best traits of our ancestors, and remind us to live up to them and celebrate them.

4. Friendship Group Stories

Friendship group stories are the ones we tell again and again when we reunite with old friends. Such stories preserve group cohesiveness, reminding members of their history together, and preventing them from getting too big for their britches. You might be a doctor, a lawyer, or a successful business owner now, but your best friend from junior high will always know and remember who you were, including the time you got kicked out of cranky old Mrs. Smart's English class!

5. Cultural Stories

Cultural stories transmit values and beliefs from one generation to the next in easily grasped, easily remembered form, which is why they are generally how children are introduced to religion. In our intellectual lives and our early lives as students, stories come first. Only much later do we learn actively to reflect upon and analyze the narratives of which our lives our woven.

6. Social Stories

Social storytelling is a politically correct way of saying 'gossip.' Gossip has a negative reputation because it usually involves the mean-spirited spreading of rumors and talking badly about someone behind their back. Most tragically, gossiping destroys trust. When you are in a gathering and someone starts gossiping about one who is not there, as soon as the gathering concludes, everybody leaves wondering what that person is going to say about them when they are not around! We must always be loyal to those who are not present.

7. Urban Myths and Legends

Urban myths and legends are sometimes also known as 'apocryphal' stories, from a Greek root meaning, 'to hide.' These are stories of doubtful authenticity that are nearly always presented as true, as in 'This really happened to my best friend's girlfriend's cousin, so I know it's true!' Generally, these are stories about things we fear or things we don't fully understand. Sometimes, they give us an opportunity to triumph over our fears; sometimes, they serve as reminders of what we should fear.

8. Phenomenon

Stories of angels, near-death experiences, ghosts, haunted houses, UFOs, angels, ESP, Deja vu, and the like are all very appealing. Why?

There are three potential reasons: they allow us to be frightened but at a safe distance; they offer explanations for things we don't really understand; and they can make life seem richer and more meaningful.

9. Organizational Storytelling

We must identify why our organization exists, what is its primary purpose, and why we choose to work in it and on it. This is where the 'story' and storytelling come into the equation for creating or sustaining your chosen organizational culture of significance. Let me explain:

Though rarely appearing in a job description, understanding and tapping the power of stories effectively and ethically are vital tasks for senior managers and leaders in organizations. The spoken word brings people into each other's presence. A good story not only engages the imagination of the listener and reveals far more than the words alone but during this intimate exchange, the teller and listener meet each other in a profoundly human way.

Six Benefits of Telling Organizational Stories

1. Teaching Ethical Principles with Humor

Message Joke: "Reputation Matters"

A young soldier was working in the army supply building when he answered a telephone call. "Inventory check," the deep voice demanded.

The soldier reported, "We have 1500 rifles, 10 tanks, and one fat-headed sergeant's Jeep."

The voice on the other end said, "What?"

The soldier repeated, "We have 1500 rifles, 10 tanks, and one fat-headed sergeant's Jeep."

Angrily, the voice asked, "Do you know who this is?"

The soldier replied, "No."

"This is the Sergeant!"

The soldier gasped, "Whoa. Do you know who this is?"

The Sergeant answered, "No."

The soldier yelled, "Good. Bye, bye, fathead!"

Message Joke: "Lead From The Front"

A young Army General finally got a chance to meet a famous older General who had never lost a battle. When the young General asked him what his secret was, the older General explained, "I always led my men into battle, marching at the front of the line wearing a bright red shirt."

Perplexed, the young General observed, "But didn't that make you a target?"

The older General answered, "Yes. But when I got shot, the red color of my blood meshed perfectly into the red color of my shirt and my men never knew I had been shot. So they kept fighting until we won the battle. You should try it."

The young General replied, "Thanks. I will. Lieutenant, will you please bring me my brown pants?"

2. Communicating Vision and Purpose

When individual leaders and executive teams tell authentic stories, they communicate vision and purpose in what we call 'Narrative Leadership,' which touches the hearts and minds of those who they lead in a unique influential way.

In Dr. Martin Luther King's famous speech, he did not present a five-point plan for improving race relations. Instead, he told the story of his dream of a time when black children and white children would be judged not by the color of their skin but by their character and abilities.

3. Imagining Future Possibilities

Conventional strategic planning attempts to forecast the future rationally and determine the steps to be taken toward a particular goal. But we can only put energy into what we can imagine. Story techniques offer another perspective, enabling us to take an imaginative leap into a future from which we can 'back-cast' to see the steps that will have been taken to reach there. The richer the picture and the more evocative the story, the more it can help bring that future into being.

4. Diagnosing Changing Culture

Organizational cultural change is a process that begins and is sustained when personal and organizational stories are shared that reveal the behaviors, values, beliefs, and assumptions that actively constitute the culture and the contradictions between what is espoused and what gets enacted day-to-day. When we understand that our organizational culture is grounded in the shared experiences of their people, telling these stories changes the nature of conversation in the organization and creates a level of personal authenticity that builds and strengthens trust.

5. Working With Conflict

When we are stuck in conflict or caught up in the same old bind, we can gain perspective and leverage on the problem by using stories to step outside the immediate situation. Through stories, we can acknowledge outdated ways of being and doing things and fictionalize real characters and situations to open up new possibilities for action and conflict resolution without calling anybody 'out' or stepping on anyone's toes.

6. Building Effective Teams

In organizations where time is scarce and the pressure to perform is intense, we sometimes try to accelerate this process by holding management retreats. But all too often the results are shallow and transitory. One of the enduring ways we create communities is by sharing personal stories, which enable everyone to have a voice and participate in writing the newest chapters of the organizational book. Remember, we support that which we help create.

Chapter Seventeen

Eleven Elements for Writing/Telling Significant Stories

(Embellished Overview)

"There are only 12 notes in music. Every song written in every genre was written with these same 12 notes. The only difference between one song and another is the order in which you place the notes and the timing and spacing between them. Because all songwriters have access to the same information and the same verse, verse, chorus, bridge, chorus formula,' the only difference between a hit songwriter and a lousy songwriter is passion, creativity, and imagination!" – Dan Clark

The goal of a speaker and an author is to connect with our audience and readers, seeking to bless not impress. Therefore, it is critical to always include at least one amazing story in every point of our speech and in every chapter of our book – even if it's only an amusing experience.

The following is a comprehensive list of ways in which successfully published authors and Hall of Fame speakers transform our writing into significant, incredible, memorable stories:

1. Get Inspired

If you want to be able to write a good short story, or even a long one, then you must keep your eyes and ears open at all times. Listen to the world and let it inspire you! You will soon find out what you can write about to make the best story.

When you pay attention to your surroundings and listen to people talk, you should also pay attention not only to the realities of the world but to the possibilities, asking, 'What if it happened like this instead?' or 'What would this person do if...' This will trigger your passion, creativity, and imagination and help reveal your deepest thoughts, which in turn, motivate you to explore the mysteries that are fascinating enough for you to write about.

Notice interesting character traits in others. Seek to know the mindset of champions and what allowed them to overcome obstacles and rise to the occasion. Then present your 'insider information' in a way that illuminates your unique take on what 'really' happened.

2. Elicit Emotion

Throughout this entire book, we have reiterated the significance of beginning every writing session with the clear understanding that 'reason leads to conclusions, but it is emotion that leads to action.' Readers and listeners remember how you made them feel more than what you said! The effectiveness of using emotion is predicated on the author/storyteller's ability to select the right emotion that not only embodies your main character: joy, sadness, anger, fear, confusion, depression, hunger, loneliness, fatigue, stress, disgust, happiness, and surprise – but it reveals how your character best displays that emotion, why and how he/she has been impacted by the events that occurred in the story, and rewards the reader/listener for investing the time and energy required to finish the story and embrace the message.

3. Develop your Plot

Every short story should have a plot that grips the reader and the listener, leading him to ask what will happen next. The secret to writing an amazing, thought-provoking, page-turning, engaging plot is to always keep the stakes of the story clear. Any reader and audience member should be able to answer, "What's at stake?" while he's reading or listening to your story, and after he's done. If a reader and listener gets to the end of the story and has no idea what was at stake, then the story has failed.

4. Create Suspense and Drama

To create suspense, set up a dramatic question like, "Is he going to make it?" or "Is she going to get the man of her dreams?" By putting your protagonist's fate in doubt, you make the reader ask, "What happens next?" You can also create suspense and drama by writing and speaking about death, which is a universal theme because every person who lives will one day die. The secret is to never leave them at this low melancholy point for too long by immediately helping them out of it with a positive message such as: 'Everyone dies, the old will, the young may. But not everyone truly lives! Will you leave no regrets?'

5. Develop your Characters

Your story must have a character or characters that your readers and listeners can relate to and care about and cheer on, even if the characters aren't upstanding citizens or good-natured people. The characters are the mouthpiece of the writer and speaker to carry out the plot of the story, which requires that you:

- Describe what they say and how they interact with others – shy, domineering? The perfect line of dialogue can shed insight into a character's intentions.

- Describe what they do – habits, routines, job

- Describe what they look like - hair, size, wardrobe

- Remember to illuminate the Law of Attraction by linking your characters to the specific emotion you chose to convey, which causes your characters to send out energy and vibration on a specific frequency

6. Create Conflict Between a Protagonist and Antagonist

There must be something at stake in every story, or the reader won't want to keep reading. Every story needs conflict or a point of tension so your readers and listeners care what happens. You accomplish this by creating *a Protagonist and an Antagonist.*

The Protagonist represents your personal opinion on the subject and is your voice for teaching your truth. He/she is the good, noble person every reader and audience member can root for, who wins and rides off into the sunset because good always prevails over evil or the story fails and the conclusion of the story has no conclusion.

The Antagonist is the archetype villain, the protagonist's opposite with a point of view that readers and listeners sympathize with, who engages in a war of ideals and words with your protagonist.

7. Develop your Setting

When did your story happen? What is the environmental backdrop: village, city, countryside, home? From whose eyes is the audience going to see the story? Make sure you transport your audience to a different time and place so they can connect emotionally with your tale. Remember that places and environments, like people, have a specific energy and vibration that a great writer and storyteller brings to life.

8. Develop your Point-of-View

Most short stories are written and delivered in first, second or third person:

- First-person narrative is told directly from the perspective of a character who uses "I" to refer to himself. "I've never told anyone this before."

- Second-person narrative addresses the reader directly as "you," as in, "You are walking into your office."
- The third-person narrative is when you write about a character using "he" or "she" from an outside perspective, such as saying, "He was tired."

9. Develop your Dialogue

Dialogue marks the words that characters say - words and slang phrases that sound like they can be spoken by real people instead of sounding too fancy or forced, creating an exchange of energy and vibration on an interactive frequency of emotion.

10. Insert Emotion in Pivotal Spots

To captivate readers/listeners and guarantee they retain your message, it is critical to take them on an emotional roller coaster ride that makes them remember your words! This is accomplished by itemizing the pivotal moments in the story where you can evoke emotion, and then taking the required time to paint a 'heart-wrenching word picture' that makes that moment come alive!

Story: "World Champion Mindset and Skillset"

In the 1988 Olympic Winter Games I was fascinated by the back story of one amazing athlete.

The story began in 1987, when U.S. speed skater Dan Jansen's sister Jane, who was also a speed skater, was diagnosed with leukemia. Inspired by her relentless battle to live, Dan won three gold medals at the World Championships held in Milwaukee just two weeks before the 1988 Calgary Olympic Games.

But seven hours before the biggest race of his career, Dan received word that his sweet sister had passed away. Despite his inconceivable sorrow, he resolved he would win for Jane, determined to live up to everyone's expectations and capture the gold.

Lining up for the 500-meter sprint against Japan's Yasushi Kuroiwa, Jansen adjusted the hood on his sleek racing suit and took a deep breath. Clearly, his body was there but not his mind or his heart.

As usual, he busted out of the starting blocks, but in the first turn suddenly and shockingly fell and skidded violently into the padded wall—a heartbreaking scene of agony. With the world watching, he slowly rose from the ice and skated toward the side of the oval. Feeling he had let his sister down, he buried his face in his hands.

In the following 1000-meter race, he fell again. In 1992, at Albertville, France, he placed fourth in the 500-meter and an embarrassing twenty-sixth in the 1000-meter. Despite these disappointments, Jansen continued to persevere and stretch himself in his training, retaining his place on the U.S. Olympic team for the 1994 games.

In the 500-meter race, he slipped momentarily, avoiding a fall but losing enough time to wind up in eighth place. In the 1000-meter race, his last Olympic event and his last race ever, Jansen finally won a gold medal, establishing a world-record time of 1 minute 12.43 seconds.

Jansen's coach, Dr. Jim Loehr, revealed that the reason Dan was finally able to win that elusive Olympic gold was that he had developed an emotional focus on the moment. What Jansen needed to do was focus on every 'right now.' Technically, it was 'one foot in front of the other.' Mentally, it was to maintain feelings of gratitude for all the years the sport had given him.

11. Ignite All Five Senses

The most powerful and mesmerizing way to take your storytelling to its maximum connective level is to engage your readers/listeners in the five senses: touch, sight, hearing, smell, and taste. This is achieved by using physical references that deepen your characterizations, creating texture and depth to your work with shapes and colors, so we sense how the characters think and feel in any given situation.

Chapter Eighteen

Ten More Elements for Writing/Telling Significant Stories

(Continuation of Embellished Overview)

12. Be True to Your Self

Because our listeners and readers relate to our failures and imperfections more than our successes and perfections, it is vital that we as storytellers are authentically vulnerable and real in sharing our limiting beliefs, the agony of defeat, and our breakthrough moments and thrills in victory.

Too many authors and speakers dumb down their work and significance because they're afraid of alienating the majority of customers and audience members they imagine they should be writing for and speaking to. Don't do it! If your readers and meeting-goers like to read the sorts of books you like to read, they will definitely like the same things you share in your stories, books, and speeches.

13. Don't 'Re-Tell' the Story. 'Re-Live' It

Invite readers/listeners into the experience so they see themselves as the Characters. For example, suppose I tell the story of sixteen-year-old Mary Lou Retton scoring a perfect 10 as a gymnast in the final floor exercise and vault competitions in the 1984 Olympics to win the Gold medal for her team. In that case, I am merely entertaining and inspiring my listeners. However, if I also include the countless times in practice when she flew off the bars and crashed and burned on her beam, vault, and tumbling routines when her toes bled, and the tears streamed down her face – I take the listeners from 'look what she has done' to 'you can do it too.'

If you act out the flips and swings and falls and animate the dismounts it makes the story come alive with the intellectually and emotionally stimulating questions: 'What if Mary Lou had quit after the first ten crashes, never realizing that she was just one crash away from perfecting that one element of her entire routine that would eventually make her world champion? Will you quit before you succeed?'

14. Be Witty

What readers and listeners love above all is humor, wit, and frivolity. Note that it is not telling a joke that takes no intelligence to perceive. Wit is more of a brain thing that showcases we are not just putting on a show, but rather carrying on an inspirational conversation telling real stories, and being authentically present in the moment. Wit makes us laugh because we're surprised or caught off guard by believable incongruities such as the nuclear scientist who can't heat a cup of soup, the successful MBA who runs up credit card debt, and the diplomat who can't keep peace in his own house.

For example, I was intimidated when I walked on stage as a keynote speaker in front of my peers at a National Speakers Association National Convention.

So, what did I do to relieve my own tension and turn around the obvious into the humorous, unexpected, and absurd? I started my speech by saying, "I'm sure you are all sitting there a little nervous, wondering whether I am going to like you. (Ha!) Well, rest assured that we can develop a good relationship in a very short time. Last night I went through airport security and was frisked so completely we still write!" Everyone laughed and my connection to the audience was underway!

15. Inspire Them to Cry

When listeners can think and laugh and cry and laugh and cry again, experiencing a roller coaster ride through every emotion in the same speech, they remember it.

When we use humor and take our readers and listeners to a high point of laughter above the emotional medium, it gives us the right to take them to the same point of tears below the emotional medium, without them feeling manipulated or violated. The secret is to never leave them at this melancholy point for long by immediately giving them 'comic relief' that takes them back up to the medium point of emotion.

16. Use Stories the Listeners Relate To

'When in Rome, do as the Romans do.' When in Russia don't tell stories about American athletes, United States astronauts, and New York ballerinas. Tell stories about Russian sports and Olympic champions, their most famous cosmonauts, their incredible dancers, and Russian music composers. When speaking in Europe or Latin America don't tell stories about American football. Tell stories about their World Cup Soccer heroes and highlights from famous games, sharing details about which players did what, and for which team, calling them by name.

17. Take Relationships to a Vulnerable Level

One night I had to take my three-year-old daughter to the hospital. Sitting in the emergency room, I just wanted to fit in and look like and be like everyone else. A macho man came in with his son, and the physician asked about the problem. 'My boy fell down and broke his leg. Didn't even cry!' I thought, Oh, perfect.

Then a mother came in with her little girl. The physician inquired about her daughter. 'My daughter fell off the beam at the gymnastics meet and badly twisted her knee.' I thought, Oh, perfect!

Then the doctor finally asked me why I was there with my daughter. I said, 'She has a raisin stuck in her nose!' Everybody laughed. I wanted to fit in, but my little girl taught me that it's okay to be outside the lines!

18. Take Mistakes to their Sweetest Solutions

A little boy spilled cranberry juice on the new carpet in his living room. Shaking with fear and sobbing giant tears of pain, he humbly walked into the kitchen to confess.

'Mom, I'm so sorry. I just spilled my big glass of juice on your new carpet. I feel very, very bad.' His mother hugged him and said, 'It's okay. Don't be sad. We can get you another glass of cranberry juice.'

19. Take Work to its Greatest Enjoyment

As we were coming in for a landing at the Dallas/Fort Worth airport, our Delta Airlines jet hit heavy turbulence and jolted all over the sky. When we finally touched down, we bounced three times, skidded to a halt, and taxied to the terminal. On our way to the gate the flight attendant spoke over the cabin public address system: 'Welcome to Dallas, Texas. Please remain seated with your seatbelt fastened while Captain Kangaroo bounces us the rest of the way to the gate! Ha! If you enjoyed your flight, tell your friends you flew Delta Airlines. If you did not enjoy your flight, tell your friends you flew Southwest!' Haha!

20. Inspire Support

John McMaster became a superstar basketball player in high school. For each of his three years on the team, he was All-Conference, All-State. In his final season, he was named the most valuable player of the league. John's mother never missed a game, home or away, regardless of the travel distance or weather conditions. His mom was always in the bleachers cheering her son to victory. Interestingly, John's mother was totally blind! What's the message? Although the mother could not see her son, he could see her. Support makes the special difference!

21. Use the Power of 'Invitational Engagement'

Use your creativity and imagination to write the perfect concluding scenario that capsulizes the essence of your message in an action-based conclusive scenario. Therefore, I bring my stories to a head by asking questions that invite readers and listeners to decide which character in my conclusion are they playing.

A young man changes the world with a significant invention, but he admits that he was led to a life of inventing by a book he had read.

So, to whom do we owe our debt of gratitude for enriching our lives so significantly with this invention? The inventor? Or the author of the book who the inventor admits led him to a life of inventing?

Or should we thank the teacher who encouraged a child to become an author? Certainly, without the teacher, the book never would have been written.

Or are we indebted to the successful businesswoman who created the scholarship that allowed a poor, underserved girl to attend college and become the teacher who encouraged her student to become the author of the book that inspired the man whose invention changed the world?

Or should we thank the doctor who saved the life of a mother, who several years later bore the child who became the significant businesswoman who created the college scholarship?

Or maybe the one who really deserves our deepest appreciation is the hardworking delivery man who drove the wagon that carried the lumber that was used to build the doctor's office, where the doctor saved the woman who bore the child who grew up to create the scholarship that allowed the disadvantaged student to attend college and become a teacher who inspired her student to write a book that inspired the young inventor to change the world.

Every soul on earth is caught somewhere in this circle of influence! Where are you in this continuum of gratitude?

Chapter Nineteen

The Ultimate Leadership, Selling, and Marketing Language

(Embracing All 'Figures of Speech' and Eliminating Rejection Words)

"Edit so every word pays its own way!" – Dan Clark

People get so accustomed to using the same words and phrases over and over, and always in the same ways, that they no longer know what they mean. Persuasive, polished storytellers are Creative Writers who have the passion and imagination to make the ordinary strange and the strange ordinary, making life interesting again because they encourage interpretation.

When readers or listeners encounter a phrase or word that cannot be interpreted literally, they have to think - or rather, they are given the pleasure of interpretation. If you write or say "I am frustrated" or "The air was cold" you give your readers and listeners nothing to do - they say, "So what?" But if you say, "My ambition was like craving a breath of air from an underwater cave," your readers and listeners can choose many meanings.

Therefore, the very best and most compelling storytellers use Leadership Language, Metaphors, Similes, and all 'Figures of Speech so that 'Every Word Pays Its Own Way!'

Speak Like a Leader

- Instead of saying, 'I think.' Say 'I believe,' conveying conviction.
- Instead of 'I don't know.' Say 'Let's explore this,' conveying an open mind, focusing not on who is right but on what is right.
- Instead of 'I'm too busy.' Say 'I'm tied up right now, can we talk later,' displaying compassionate decisiveness.
- Instead of 'We failed.' Say 'This is a learning opportunity,' fostering growth.
- Instead of 'Good job.' Say 'I appreciate your effort,' which personalizes the feedback.
- Instead of, 'Tell me.' Say 'I'm listening,' conveying genuine interest and caring consideration.
- Instead of 'You're welcome.' Say 'My pleasure,' conveying a more sincere reason that you served them.
- Instead of 'I don't know.' Say 'Let me find out,' conveying that finding the right answer matters to you.
- Instead of 'That's impossible.' Say 'Let's find a solution,' putting emphasis on the process of change, not the promise.
- Instead of 'I hate this.' Say 'I'm not a fan of this,' conveying a sensitive respect toward a person, product, or service.
- Instead of 'I'm sorry to bother you.' Say 'Could you spare me a couple of minutes,' conveying respect for their time.
- When receiving a compliment don't just say 'Thank You.' Instead, say 'You're even better.'
- If a leader thanks you, don't say 'No Problem.' Respond with 'You are too kind. Feel free to call on me anytime.'
- When praised, accept graciously and offer a compliment in return so both parties feel good.
- When a leader praises your abilities say 'Thanks to your excellent leadership I didn't let you down.'

- Never gossip or criticize someone behind their back. To create and sustain trust we must be loyal to those who are not present.

Metaphor

Dictionary definition: "When a word or phrase is applied to an object or action to which it is not literally applicable - a thing regarded as representative or symbolic of something else - often used to connect two unlike things or to denote something from a figurative standpoint."

Metaphors are powerful tools for explaining concepts that might otherwise be difficult for people to grasp.

Imagine what would happen if instead of starting a speech with, 'Let us focus on the fundamentals and start at the beginning,' we began by sharing a 'metaphorical story.' For example:

A man had a dream where a genie came to him and explained, 'You've lived a noble life, and I will grant you one wish.' The man thought and answered, 'I wish that peace and love and prosperity fill the whole earth.' The genie replied, 'That's a noble wish sir, but we don't deal in fruits here, we only deal in seeds.'

Metaphors enliven ordinary language, are more efficient than ordinary language, give maximum meaning in fewer words, and allow us to write about difficult things more efficiently. Examples:

- "All our words are crumbs from the feast of the mind."
- "A hospital bed is a parked taxi with the meter running."
- "A good conscience is a continual Christmas."
- "Dying is a wild night on a new road." Emily Dickinson
- Time is money
- The eye is the window to the soul
- A roller coaster of emotions
- Slippery slope
- He took his ball and went home
- He was chomping at the bit to hear this news
- She danced to the beat of her own drum
- The ball is in your court

Similes

Dictionary definition: 'The comparison of one thing with another thing of a different kind, used to make a description more emphatic or vivid. Similes are distilled Metaphors, finely tuned to fewer words.' Similes make our language more descriptive and enjoyable. Poets and songwriters use them to add depth and quickly emphasize what they are conveying in a more vivid, explicit way. Examples:

- 'My heart skipped like a man running with a nail in his foot.'
- 'The air on the street smelled like the last weekend of baseball.'
- 'It's like trying to do trigonometry with someone kicking your head.'
- 'The slivered moon hung low in the sky like an afterthought.'
- 'The orange sun is rolling across the sky like a severed head.'
- 'His smile was so wide he could have eaten a banana sideways.'
- busy as a bee
- blind as a bat
- big as a house
- thin as a rail
- tough as nails
- strong as an ox
- easy as shooting fish in a barrel
- different as night and day

Other 'Figures of Speech'

Analogies is a comparison of two things to describe their similarities as in: finding a good man is like finding a needle in a haystack; life is like a box of chocolates – you never know what you're gonna get.

Imagery is the use of vivid language to create mental images of objects, actions, or ideas such as 'A Racer who had dinner plate patches of flesh torn away by 60-mile-per-hour crashes; 'his smile was so wide he could have eaten a banana sideways.'

Denotation is the dictionary or literal meaning of a word as in: 'courage is the quality of being brave.'

Connotative is the association to emotions triggered by a word or phrase as in: 'One Racer suffered a broken nose and still he continued.'

Parallelism is the similar arrangement of a pair or series of related words phrases or sentences as in: 'prim and proper,' 'cool, calm, and collected.'

Reiteration is the repeating of a clause or phrase: 'I have a dream, I have a dream.'

Personification is attributing human characteristics to an inanimate object such as 'time flies; the camera lovers her; my alarm clock yells at me; the pie is calling my name.'

Sales and Marketing 'Rejection Words'

Zig Ziglar taught, 'The sale doesn't begin until the customer says no.' And 'no' is usually a result of the words the sales professional uses that cause a prospect to reject an idea, product, or service.

- Nobody likes to be 'Sold.' We like to 'Own.' If I want it, I will take it.

- Never use the word 'Price.' It creates the thought that 'maybe I should shop around and find a better deal and lower price.' Instead, use 'Total Investment.'

- Never use 'Down Payment.' Instead, use 'Initial Investment'

- Never use 'Contract.' Use 'Agreement,' 'Paperwork' or 'Form.'

- Never use 'Sign.' Use 'Endorse', ' Authorize', 'Approve', or 'Fill Out the Form.'

- Never use 'Buy.' Use 'Invest,' or 'Own' – nobody wants to buy - we want to own it.

- Never use 'Sold.' Use 'Get Them Involved' or 'Help Them Acquire.'

- Never use 'Objections.' Use 'Area of Concern.'

- Never use 'Deal.' Use 'Opportunity' or 'Transaction.'

- Never use 'Problem.' Use 'Challenge.'

In Marketing

- Don't use 'Discount.' They will leave and check other options.
- Don't say 'Sign Up.' Say 'Join the Movement.'
- Don't say 'Best.' Say 'Top Rated.'
- Don't say 'Buy Now.' Say 'Start Your Journey.'
- Don't say 'Affordable.' Say 'High Value.'
- Don't say 'Newest.' Say 'Revolutionary.'
- If you are the 'Cheapest,' no one expects you to be the 'Best.' If you are the 'Best,' no one expects you to be the "Cheapest!'

Story: "Price Verses Cost"

The difference between price and cost is discovered when a dad takes his son to the Schwinn shop to buy him a new bike. The price tag is $100, so the dad goes to a discount store, where a salesman convinces him to buy a cheaply made bike for only $50.

Two weeks later the seat wiggles loose and needs to be repaired. Because there is no warranty, the dad is charged $20 for the repair. Two weeks later the handlebars bend down, the bearings in the back wheel freeze up and the chain breaks, forcing the dad back to the store to pay another $60 in repairs.

Dad complains, scolding the owner for selling him a lemon, angrily pays the bill, and storms out! Two weeks later, the other wheel seizes up, and angrily Dad throws the bike in the trash and buys the Schwinn he should have purchased in the first place.

Although the 'price' of the cheap bike was only $50, in just six weeks the 'cost' of that bike had risen to $130! The price of the Schwinn was $100, but because it was well-built, the son rode it for ten years with no additional cost. Price is a one-time thing. Cost is a lifetime thing. Pay me now, or pay me later! In sales and marketing, if money becomes the topic of conversation, it means the presentation is weak and the relationship is non-existent!

Chapter Twenty

The Art of Persuasion: Ethos, Pathos, Logos, Mythos

(Motivator, Healer, Shocker, or Soother)

"Don't raise your voice, improve your argument. People almost invariably arrive at their beliefs not based on proof, but on the basis of what they find attractive." – Blaise Pascal

Persuasion is defined as the act of trying to convince someone of something or the means of convincing someone to do something – using every possible technique, communication tool, and delivery system to list the reasons why you should do something. To improve our knowledge and accelerate our ability to persuade, we all must first become brilliant at the basics!

Ethos, Pathos, and Logos represent the beginning, middle, and end of a good speech.

Every great speech has an attention-grabbing opening, at least one middle qualifier, and a memorable close. From a humorous perspective, here are three of my favorites:

Opening: When they were trying to find someone to give this speech, they phoned the best-looking, most dashing, debonair man they knew. He turned them down. So, they phoned the most intelligent, educated, brilliant genius they knew. He turned them down, too. So, they asked the sweetest, most humble, sincere guy they had ever met. Hey, I couldn't turn them down three times in a row, so here I am!

Middle: I heard a speaker once say, 'We become what we think about.' This is not true. If it were true, I would have been a racehorse by the time I was twelve years old!

Close: I challenge you to drink, steal, swear, and lie. Drink from the fountain of truth, knowledge, and wisdom. Steal a little time each day to do something special for someone when you know you won't get the credit. Swear to make this the best day of your life so far. It may be your last. And when you lay down tonight, thank that God above that you are free to dream mighty dreams and make them come true!

Ethos

On a serious note, Ethos signifies a person's character. Establishing your character is the preliminary step in any attempt at persuasion. Ethos means others listen to you because they sense that what you have to say is worth listening to. They sense you can be trusted for your honesty and goodwill and know what you are talking about. Of the three factors of persuasion, Ethos should always come first.

Unless you have established your credibility as a speaker and made yourself attractive to your listeners, you will not sustain their attention, much less inspire them to do anything. For this reason, a great story must always begin with a great opening line!

Pathos

Whereas Ethos consists of the establishment of the speaker's credibility and credentials (his or her respectable and admirable character), Pathos consists of arousing the passions of the listeners and getting their emotions running in the direction of the action to be taken. Pathos is the motivating factor. This is why you must continue to sprinkle great one-liners throughout the story.

Logos

Logos is the marshaling of reason and must come last. In speaking, it does you no good to give reasons and arguments until you have first established an emotional mood that is receptive to them. In other words, it is critical to first arouse favorable feelings toward your own person and feelings in favor of the end result you are seeking before you can reinforce the feelings with your list of whys.

Reasons and arguments have no force unless your listeners are already disposed emotionally to move in the direction that your reasons justify. This could include a powerful catchy one-liner that capsulizes your entire message into a single thought and challenge so the reader/listener feels closure and leaves your speech with a consolidated challenge such as: 'Eternity is the wrong thing to be wrong about.'

All in all, Ethos epitomizes the reasons. Logos is the action to be taken by your listeners, and it confirms the feelings. Pathos is what you have already aroused. With Ethos and Pathos fully operative, Logos remains the winning trump card in the persuader's hand.

Mythos

An argument based on tradition, values of a group or identity that challenges the status quo in an even bold, politically incorrect way. Here is where you can deflect the controversial message to a third-party experience so it's not your opinion, you are simply reporting the facts.

Story: "Who is Really in Control?"

I've spent a lot of time in Russia, conducting leadership training with the United Nations, where although they don't claim to be communists, they still only have one television station in the entire country - Moscow One - 100% owned and operated by the government. Alarming is the fact that it's the most highly guarded and fortified building in all of Moscow.

The White House, Kremlin, and all other government buildings are merely guarded by a few soldiers.

However, the television station is protected by four army tanks, three stories of barbed wire fencing, a minefield, a machine gun nest and AK 47-carrying soldiers patrolling the walled fortress.

Why? He/she who controls the hearts and minds of the people controls the people! Furthermore, when I was interviewed, I realized he/she who asks the questions is in complete control of the conversation. So, should we not honestly evaluate our current media situation in America and determine if our news and social media accounts are being censured and controlled and for what purpose?

Speaker/Story Seller As 'Healer'

We all know that doctors can't and don't heal anyone. Through the administration of medication and the performance of surgery, they help us heal ourselves. Therefore, there are two kinds of healing - Healing by First Intention and Healing by Second Intention.

Healing by First Intention:

Outside healing is where there is a scratch or superficial, shallow wound with a straight edge opening that quickly coagulates, stops bleeding, and heals with a few stitches to close the cut or with just a Band-Aid to keep it clean. Name-calling, gossip, and rumors are "scuffed knees" and "paper cuts" that can and will always heal from the outside in.

Healing by Second Intention:

Inside-out healing, where the wound is deep, the edges jagged, and the gouge uncertain. In this case, if you only stop the surface bleeding, stitch the surface layer of skin, and bandage it to heal from the outside-in, underneath it all and unbeknownst to you, the wound is festering, infection is setting in, and gangrene could result in the amputation of that limb. When we suffer and experience a deep gouge wound - a stabbing, the bursting of our appendix, a broken heart, the loss of a loved one, a devastating divorce, being let go from a job - the only way we can heal is if we keep the wound open long enough with the proper treatment - kindness and care - until it can slowly, in its own time, heal from the inside-out, one layer, one step at a time.

Story Seller As 'Shocker'

When you want to help heal your audience members without sounding 'preachy' or self-righteous – especially when you are asked or feel compelled to address something as redundant as drinking and driving, which has been crammed down our throats for decades, I suggest that you use a powerful, emotionally stirring, more sharing way created in a third-party message taught through a fictitious, yet profound story:

Story: "I Can Handle It"

Steve was careful about his drinking because his wife, Melba, worried. She said liquor made him too confident and not cautious. Women never really understand their men, he thought. Instead, they always worry about things that never happen. Steve snapped up the shot glass, tilted his head, and nodded to the bartender as he left.

Outside he thought about how happy he was. Steve owned a house and Melba was pregnant again. Steve was hurrying to pick up Melba at the doctor's office. Although the car skidded slightly on the icy roads, he wanted to hurry since he'd stopped at the bar. He sped up, then suddenly realized he couldn't make the turn at the bottom of the hill.

The car was headed for the guard rail that was set around the edge of the lake. To compensate, Steve propped his door open with his briefcase so he could get out when the car hit the water. He planned to jump out and swim to the bank.

People saw the car coming and watched as it splashed into the cold lake. As he planned, Steve got out safely and swam for shore. People cheered when he arrived safely. He thought, See, I can handle my liquor.

As he stood there smiling, waving to the crowd, and watching his car submerge, Steve's heart sank. His little eighteen-month-old son, Jared, was still strapped in his car seat in the back of the car.

The Emotional Power of Music / Lyrical Poetry

The flip side of these heart-wrenching stories are inspirational songs:

"SPECIAL MAN"

A little boy wants to be like his dad
So he watches us night and day
He mimics our moves and weighs our words
He steps in our steps all the way

He's sculpting a life we're the model for
He'll follow us happy or sad
And his future depends on example set
'Cause the little boy wants to be just like his dad

A special man talks by example
Takes the time to play and hug his lad
A special man walks by example
The very best friend a growing boy ever had
Any male can be a father—
But it takes a special man to be a dad

He needs a hero to emulate
He breathes 'I believe in you.'
Would we have him see everything we see
And have him do what we do

When we see the reverence that sparkles and shines
In the worshipping eyes of our lad
Will we be at peace if his dreams come true
And he grows up to be just like his dad

"ALWAYS A REASON TO LIVE"

I've been in stormy weather
I've cried because of fears
But the soul would have no rainbows
If the eyes possessed no tears
There's always smoke with fire
And usually joy with pain
To appreciate the sunshine
You've got to have some rain

So if you're down and troubled
No matter what you do
Don't focus on the thistle
The rose will see you through
When your life is broken
It's yourself that you need to forgive
There is light at the end of the tunnel
There is always a reason to live

I've had my share of sadness
I've cried my share of tears
I've fought my way through friendships
But the real ones they last for years
I've stumbled and I've failed some
Been up yea I've been down
But I learned to soar with eagles
Though my feet are on the ground

So don't be afraid of dying
Be afraid you haven't lived
Always rise each time you fall
When your back's against the wall
Eliminate your shame
Your dreams you can reclaim

So, when your life is broken
It's yourself that you need to forgive
There is light at the end of the tunnel
There is always a reason to live!

Epilogue

A Bullet Point Recap

For over eleven years, I was a university professor teaching Public Speaking, which I affectionately call the 'Privilege of the Platform') and the Art and Science of Storytelling (which is the deepest, most intimate way in which we communicate and authentically connect in both our personal and professional relationships).

Because being the best communicator we can be is the key to climbing any corporate ladder, accepting more leadership responsibilities, and rising to the occasion in your community as a leader - with and without a title - I always start each class with a simple fundamental orientation that resets the foundational mindset and emotional heart-set of every student as they dig in and hunker down to develop their creative writing skills, learn public speaking techniques and fully immerse themselves into the art and science of storytelling:

- They say the #1 fear of people is the fear of speaking in public. I disagree! Our greatest fear is Not speaking Well in public!

- Spend more time preparing yourself to speak than you do preparing a speech. When you are prepared, you shall not fear!

- No one wants you to teach only what you know. They want you to teach who you are, what you've done, how you live!

- Seek to bless, not impress.

- Under pressure you don't rise to the occasion – you fall to the level of your training. Which means pressure is not something that is naturally there. It's created when you question your own ability. When you know what you have been trained to do, there is never any pressure. That's why you train and practice so hard.

- If you are nervous before you speak, it's because you think it's about you. But if you are excited to speak, you know it's about the audience.

- The purpose of every meeting - one-on-one, one-on-ten in a Board Room, one-on-10,000 in an arena – is to rekindle passion, unlock creativity, trigger imagination – to give the listener an experience they can't get at home or work – and take them to an intellectual and emotional place they cannot take themselves through the power of storytelling!

- Always remember that no one remembers what they hear as much as what they feel and why they feel it. Feelings created only because you took the time to become a powerful, polished storyteller that equipped and empowered you to authentically and deeply connect heart-to-heart, spirit-to-spirit, and soul-to-soul with them because of the stories you just shared!

- Tell your own stories! Be you – authentically you – you'll make a lousy somebody else!

- Most significant - you have no credibility as a speaker and 'story seller' unless you are the same off-stage as you are on stage – the same at home, school, work, and play. You can't just practice what you preach - you must preach only what you practice! You are the message!

Conclusion

This is a quick course, yet a Master Class on the Art and Science of Storytelling and the incredible power that comes when you transform it into Story Selling! Consequently, I leave you with one of my favorite stories that I've written and love to tell. It's about one of the original 'Wishes' granted by the Make-A-Wish Foundation started by a dear friend, hero, and international philanthropist Frank Shankwitz, who passed away leaving a lasting legacy! 1943-2021 (RIP). Enjoy. Feel. Laugh. Cry. Remember. Love. Serve. Donate. Grant a Wish. God bless.

Story: "Bopsy"

Bopsy was a ten-year-old boy living in Phoenix, Arizona, dying of terminal leukemia. At present, there is no cure. One day, his mother had the presence of mind to ask him, "Bopsy, if you had one wish, what would it be?" Without even thinking about it, Bopsy replied, "Mommy, if I had one wish and I knew it would come true, I'd want to be a fireman."

The next morning, Bopsy's mother phoned the local fire department and talked to the fire chief. She explained her son's health condition and his wish. The fire chief had a heart as big as a house and answered, "I'd love to make Bopsy's dream come true. You tell him that we'll be by to pick him up at 8:00 a.m. We'll make him honorary fire chief for the whole day." The fire chief continued, "If you'll give me Bopsy's measurements, I'll have a helmet made for him just like the big guys wear. We'll have a yellow slicker jacket and rubber galoshes for him too."

Sure enough, at 8:00 a.m. the fire engine pulled up in front of Bopsy's house. They helped him get all decked out in his very own fireman's uniform, and that day he got to go on two fire calls. It inspired him to the depth of his being, so that he lived three months longer than any doctor thought he could possibly live.

On the last night of Bopsy's short life, the head nurse in the hospital was monitoring his vital signs and noticed they were starting to weaken. Bopsy's parent's eyes filled with tears as they knew his short life was coming to an end. Scrambling to help in any way she could, the nurse remembered the relationship Bopsy had developed with the local fire department. Immediately she phoned the fire chief and told him, "Bopsy is not doing too good and I thought you would like to know. Maybe there is something you could do for him."

The fire chief shouted, "You tell that little guy to hang on. We will be there in five minutes. But, nurse, there are a couple of things we need you to do for us. Will you please announce over the PA system of the hospital that everyone is going to hear the sirens screaming and see the lights flashing, and that we are coming to see our boy Bopsy for the last time? And would you please open up the third-story window to Bopsy's hospital room, because this time we're coming by hook and ladder!"

Moments later the sirens were screaming, the lights were flashing, and the fire engines pulled up to the hospital. A huge ladder went up the side of the building. Ten firemen and two firewomen scampered up the ladder and climbed through the third-story window into Bopsy's hospital room. They kissed him and cuddled him. With tears streaming down everyone's cheeks, the big, burly fire chief leaned over Bopsy's hospital bed and took hold of his frail little hand. With a big smile on his precious, innocent face, Bopsy looked up at the fire chief and with his last breath asked, "Chief, am I now really a fireman?"

The fire chief answered, "Bopsy, you are." And the little guy died.

Emotional Close

Can you now see and feel why I wanted to conclude this book/course/ Master Class with a story? And when I share this story in a speech, obviously I can't leave the audience hanging or in a saddened state of pain. I must lift them back up to the significant lessons learned and send them out on a positive motivated note that goes like this:

"Is this a story about death? Or is it a story about life and the power of a dream and the significance of love and support and service? I know this story of Bopsy resonates with everyone, young and old, because each of us has a dream stuck inside still unfulfilled. So, I guess the concluding question is, "What are you going to do about your dream?" It's like they say in the movie South Pacific, "If you don't have a dream, how ya gonna make a dream come true?"

"Summarized Conclusion!"

Let me leave you with the powerful words of U.S. President Ronald Reagan. Right after he had been shot in an assassination attempt and realizing how important it is to live our lives with a sense of urgency, the President said, "America was founded on a dream, and now it's your turn to keep that dream moving. We've always reached for a new spirit and aimed at a higher goal. We've always been courageous, determined, unafraid, and bold. Who among us ever wants to say we no longer have those qualities?

"We look to you to meet the great challenge, to reach beyond the commonplace, and not fall short for lack of creativity and courage. And to do this? All you need to begin with is a dream to do better than ever before. All you need is to have faith, and that dream will come true. All you need to do is act, and the time for action is now!

I agree with President Reagan and challenge all of us to do the same! And then to document and chronicle our lives and put them into polished stories that we can share with the world!

The End
(which is the beginning!)

Make sure you take advantage of this special offer to buy Five of Dan's Best-selling Books as a companion resource set to put on your shelf next to 'Story Selling.' Remember, Dan teaches us to make every speech and story Funny (Humor File), Evocative (Treasury of Quotes), Emotional (Chicken Soup stories), and meaningful content (Art of Significance) to illustrate points and embellish the message).